S0-EJO-835

0000101909992

Sheldon Z. Kramer, PhD

Transforming the Inner and Outer Family: Humanistic and Spiritual Approachs to Mind-Body Systems Therapy

*Pre-publication
REVIEWS,
COMMENTARIES,
EVALUATIONS . . .*

" **S** heldon Kramer, building on Assagioli's psychosynthesis work, Virginia Satir's growth model, and others, creatively synthesizes eastern, holistic, and family systems approaches to healing. This important book deals with such concepts as love, compassion, understanding, joy, and forgiveness–aspects of the human condition that fluster most therapists. Particularly intriguing are Kramer's use of guided imagery, body movement, and meditation techniques in healing one's inner and outer families. We all need to know the message in this excellent, trail-blazing book."

James L. Framo, PhD
Distinguished Professor,
United States International University,
San Diego, CA

More pre-publication
REVIEWS, COMMENTARIES, EVALUATIONS . . .

"**D**r. Sheldon Kramer magnificently integrates both the conceptual and practical aspect of life into the mainstream of personhood and everyday human growth. His book is especially timely for the therapeutic profession–be it psychiatry, family therapy, social work, psychology, or medical practice."

John Banmen, RPsych
Psychologist and Family Therapist;
Faculty, University
of British Columbia;
Co-Author, The Satir Model:
Family Therapy and Beyond

"**K**ramer is a people-maker's people-maker. He gives not only the *what* of transformation but even more importantly the *how*. His essential contribution is in making the spiritual dimension visible and the spiritual tools accessible."

Zalman M. Schachter-Shalomi
Aleph Alliance for Jewish Renewal;
Author, *Paradigm Shift*
and *Spiritual Intimacy*

"**S**heldon Kramer's book is an outstanding intellectual and aesthetic contribution to the field of psychotherapy. The author writes clearly and illustrates his work with detailed clinical illustrations, thus making his book a real instructional tool for therapists at all levels of experience. Even those who are normally frightened away by matters of spirit and want their science and practice toughly grounded in empirical realities will be drawn deeply into this work. This book is a cogent and clear detailing of realizable procedures for accessing inner parts of the personality and the mind that obviously underlie both many strong emotional patterns as well as determining cognitive paradigms.

One should note that his book is also a gift to those who loved Virginia Satir: Kramer draws deeply on her work as well as presents the reader with gifts of verbatim dialogues with Satir in the period just before her death."

Israel W. Charny, PhD
Professor of Psychology
& Family Therapy and Director,
Program for Advanced Studies
in Integrative Psychotherapy,
Hebrew University of Jerusalem

More pre-publication
REVIEWS, COMMENTARIES, EVALUATIONS . . .

"**W**ith this excellent book, Sheldon Kramer has made an important contribution both to the field of family therapy and psychosynthesis. Regarding the former, he has developed a methodologically accurate, well-balanced, pragmatic integration of the humanistic and transpersonal dimensions with the systemic family approach. In psychosynthesis, he has filled a gap by introducing an organized body of theory and practice of psychosynthetic family psychotherapy.

Highly recommendable to all psychotherapists and professionals working with couples and families, this clearly written volume also makes pleasant reading for the interested non-professional. It is certainly valuable for anyone wishing to increase that sensitivity and potential necessary in the healing journey through relationships."

Massimo Rosselli, MD
Psychiatrist;
President, Italian Society
of Therapeutic Psychosynthesis

"**D**r. Kramer has written a powerful, practical guide on how to heal our emotional wounds and become whole, to make peace simultaneously with ourselves and our families, and to integrate the sacred through the challenges of intimate relationships. I especially appreciate the processes for family meditation, mobilizing the will, and healing intergenerational wounds."

Harold H. Bloomfield, MD
Psychiatrist;
Author, *Making Peach with Your Family* and *Power of Five*

"**D**r. Kramer demonstrates the value of looking at human beings as dynamic fields of energy and information, continuously aiming to extract nourishment from their environments. Family therapists who embrace the author's insights will be more effective healers to their clients and themselves."

David Simon, PhD
Medical Director, Sharp Institute
for Human Potential and Mind-Body
Medicine, San Diego, CA

More pre-publication
REVIEWS, COMMENTARIES, EVALUATIONS . . .

"**P**sychosynthesis focuses on the depth and beauty of each individual's inner world. But we are all part of the same living web, and there is no true understanding of an individual apart from his or her relationships. Sheldon Kramer's book is a basic contribution to this understanding as well as a helpful tool for the professional."

Piero Ferrucci
Director, Center of Study
of Psychosynthesis,
Florence, Italy;
former student and collaborator
of Roberto Assagioli

"**T**his book addresses one of the most crucial needs of our time–how to heal and strengthen the family. Like a skillful guide, Sheldon Kramer leads us beyond 'mere psychology' into humanistic and spiritual dimensions, without which healing is not possible. An important contribution, highly recommended."

Larry Dossey, MD
Author, *Healing Words;*
Meaning & Medicine; Recovering the
Soul; and *Space, Time & Medicine*

"**P**sychological therapists are fortunate to have the wonderful contribution that Sheldon Kramer is making in this book. He gives us clear, insightful ways to bring health to the whole family. Reading this book is a must for all psychologists, psychiatrists, social workers, parents, teachers, and all who want to be free within themselves."

Edith R. Stauffer, PhD
Founder/Director,
Psychosynthesis International,
Ojai, CA

"**I**n contrast to those family therapists who downplay the internal processes of the individual and those therapists who emphasize the individual and ignore the family, Sheldon Kramer brings them together into a unified system that explores healing in the context of our inner and outer relationship systems. Kramer supplements guided meditation and breathing exercises with connecting emotionally with the client–'the essential glue that helps to heal the deep psychic wounds' and that creates a deep trust between the therapist and clients."

Maurice Friedman, PhD
Co-Director, Institute
for Dialogical Psychotherapy;
Author, *The Healing Dialogue*
in Psychotherapy

More pre-publication
REVIEWS, COMMENTARIES, EVALUATIONS . . .

"**D**r. Kramer has written a much-needed, informative, and useful book for professionals, teachers, and students of family therapy, who have often expressed to me that they have been looking for a book with this focus. The author has developed very practical connections between the work of his teachers Satir and Assagioli, honoring his indebtedness and great respect for their work with numerous quotes.

The reader can find rich details in Dr. Kramer's concrete examples of his own therapy work, where he successfully bridges many different aspects and healing principles such as: individual and systemic healing models, humanistic and spiritual dimensions, meditation, guided imagery, and the use of subpersonalities."

Aric Bodin, EdD
Therapist,
Professor of Therapy,
JFK University

"**S**heldon Z. Kramer has introduced humanistic and spiritual dimensions in the field of family therapy. Spirituality, a neglected subject for many schools of psychotherapy, is described beautifully in this book through many touching examples. The use of self (body and mind in action) of the therapist is described as the major tool for producing individual and family healing. This volume honors the memory of Roberto Assagioli, the inventor of Psychosynthesis, and of Virginia Satir, the master of family healing, but it also expands their ideas. Kramer gently pushes the field to include the aesthetic dimensions in the training of family therapists."

Maurizio Andolfi, MD
Professor of Psychology,
University of Rome

The Haworth Press, Inc.

NOTES FOR PROFESSIONAL LIBRARIANS AND LIBRARY USERS

This is an original book title published by The Haworth Press, Inc. Unless otherwise noted in specific chapters with attribution, materials in this book have not been previously published elsewhere in any format or language.

CONSERVATION AND PRESERVATION NOTES

All books published by The Haworth Press, Inc. and its imprints are printed on certified ph neutral, acid free book grade paper. This paper meets the minimum requirements of American National Standard for Information Sciences–Permanence of Paper for Printed Material, ANSI Z39.48-1984.

Transforming the Inner and Outer Family

Humanistic and Spiritual Approaches to Mind-Body Systems Therapy

HAWORTH Psychotherapy
E. Mark Stern, PhD
Senior Editor

New, Recent, and Forthcoming Titles:

Families and the Interpretation of Dreams: Awakening the Intimate Web by Edward Bruce Bynum

Transcending Psychoneurotic Disturbances: New Approaches in Psychospirituality and Personality Development by Edward Bruce Bynum

Transforming the Inner and Outer Family: Humanistic and Spiritual Approaches to Mind-Body Systems Therapy by Sheldon Z. Kramer

Transforming the Inner and Outer Family
Humanistic and Spiritual Approaches to Mind-Body Systems Therapy

Sheldon Z. Kramer, PhD

NO LONGER PROPERTY OF
SEATTLE PACIFIC UNIVERSITY LIBRARY

The Haworth Press
New York • London

SEATTLE PACIFIC UNIVERSITY LIBRARY

© 1995 by The Haworth Press, Inc. All rights reserved. No part of this work may be reproduced or utilized in any form or by any means, electronic or mechanical, including photocopying, microfilm and recording, or by any information storage and retrieval system, without permission in writing from the publisher. Printed in the United States of America.

The Haworth Press, Inc., 10 Alice Street, Binghamton, NY 13904-1580

Library of Congress Cataloging-in-Publication Data

Kramer, Sheldon Z.
    Transforming the inner and outer family : humanistic and spiritual approaches to mind-body systems therapy / Sheldon Z. Kramer.
       p.   cm.
    Includes bibliographical references and index.
    ISBN 1-56024-947-1.
    1. Psychosynthesis. 2. Family psychotherapy. I. Title.
RC489.P76K73 1994
616.89′156–dc20
                                          94-47538
                                             CIP

This book is a tribute to all teachers and sages throughout time who blessed us with the ability to discover for ourselves the deepest wisdom that exists within the universe.

This volume is in honor of the memory of Roberto Assagioli and Virginia Satir, who are considered by many as contemporary sages of this period of time in our natural evolution as human beings.

This work is dedicated to my wife, Carmela, who has helped me ground my spirituality through relationship in everyday life. To my beautiful, joyous daughter, Gabriela, may you reach your highest potential and help the world evolve.

Finally, this work is dedicated to my mother, Reba Kramer, my father, Bernard H. Kramer (may he rest in peace), my brother, Dr. Mark S. Kramer, and all of my other family members, friends, colleagues, teachers, students, and patients who help continue to facilitate my own understanding of what it means to be more fully human.

I would like to thank all of the students at the United States International University in San Diego who helped to transcribe from audio/video tapes all of the collaborative classes between Virginia Satir and myself to help with certain sections of the manuscript. Some of the students who did the bulk of this work include Jean McClean, Carolyn Wright, Carolyn Jacobs, Pamela Duffy, Elisa Peck, Bobbie Paul, Sharon Faff, Brenda Scott-Mead, and Gloria Diniz.

ABOUT THE AUTHOR

Sheldon Z. Kramer, PhD, a licensed clinical psychologist in full-time private practice, is Clinical Instructor at UCSD Medical School in San Diego and Medical Consultant to Balboa Naval Hospital, where he trains psychiatry residents in family therapy. He is an adjunct faculty member at the University of Humanistic Studies in Del Mar, California, at Hebrew University in Jerusalem, Israel, and at the Psychosynthesis Institute in Florence, Italy. Dr. Kramer is Director of the Institute for Transformations and gives workshops throughout the United States, Europe, and Israel on integrating the healing of individuals within their relationship systems, with special emphasis on coordinating meditation and spirituality to his work with individuals, couples, and families.

How to Use the Book

A GUIDE FOR PROFESSIONALS AND THE GENERAL READER

For Professionals

This book was written as a guide and text for general medical and mental health professionals, trainers of psychotherapists, and for students of the helping professions. I recommend that professionals read the whole volume, particularly the more academic chapters that focus on the theoretical development of this work: Chapters 3, 4, and 5. Practical methods for mind/body systems therapies can be found in Chapters 6 through 13. Chapter 14 is about self-development that therapists themselves need to go through to be truly effective in the kind of healing work described here.

Throughout the book you will find excerpts of conversations I had with Virginia Satir concerning the processes I describe here. In particular, the Introduction to Chapter 1 is a dialogue I had with Satir on healing and spirituality. That conversation will interest professionals who want to know about her ideas and work in the last months of her life. Similarly, Chapter 15 "Epilogue," besides summarizing the book, also contains a meditation Virginia Satir often used in her work.

In Appendix I you will find a candid interview I did with Virginia Satir about her personal and professional life nine months before she died. Appendix II is a special self-help guide that can be used personally or professionally to facilitate the deepening of your client's or your own relationship journey.

For the General Reader

This volume was written for both general readers and helping professionals to provide concepts and practical tools for achieving psychological and spiritual transformation through relationships. You will receive a detailed picture of what goes on behind closed doors in a psychotherapist's intensive healing work. Through reading the whole volume, you can understand how a psychotherapist quickly achieves individual, couples, and family transformation. Many case studies I present will help to achieve a deeper understanding of this process on a practical level, which I call mind-body systems therapy.

This book was written to honor the late Virginia Satir, family therapy pioneer, who was well known throughout the world to both professionals and nonprofessionals. Many thousands of readers already know her popular book entitled, *Peoplemaking*, as well as many other books she wrote for those interested in personal growth. This book contains conversations that I had with Virginia on the topics of healing, spirituality, and relationship transformation which will reveal the valuable links between her work and mine.

In particular, Chapter 1, "Introduction: Reflections on Healing and Spirituality," contains conversations I had with Virginia Satir concerning the sacred dimensions of relationships. Chapter 2, "Healing Relationships," also can easily be read by a nonprofessional. Chapters 3, 4, and 5 are written more directly for the professional and contain theoretical material found in the field of individual, couples, and family psychotherapy. However, in Chapter 3, I recommend that you read the section, Roberto Assagioli and Psychosynthesis: Bridging Humanism with Spirituality (page 22), and in Chapter 4, the section called The Inner Family (page 29). All of Chapter 5 can easily be understood by the general reader. Chapters 6, 7, and 8 include special ways of understanding stages of intensive healing encounters. These sections could be useful for the nonprofessional to read, especially in conjunction with Appendix II, which is written specifically for the nonprofessional. It is a self-help guide of mind-body relationship tools, describing a step-by-step approach to achieving intimacy and spirituality with our loved ones. It would be best to audiotape these exercises for your own use. Chapters 9,

10, 11, 12, and 13 are case studies using mind-body systems therapy. These chapters are important because they illustrate how this process works on a day-to-day basis, for both the therapist and clients. In addition, Chapter 15, "Epilogue," includes a very profound meditation by Virginia Satir, which you might also want to audiotape for your own use.

I would like to thank all of you who read this volume, and I look forward to any comments you have about this kind of work. I welcome any kind of dialogue.

I wish you a fulfilling relationship journey!

Sheldon Z. Kramer, PhD
San Diego, California

You can reach Dr. Sheldon Z. Kramer for more information about workshops, audio and video tapes, or other information at the address below:

Institute for Transformations
2615 Camino Del Rio South, Suite 300
San Diego, California 92108, USA
Telephone/Fax 619-291-4465

CONTENTS

Foreword

This volume reflects many years of personal and professional searching for knowledge with the aim of increasing my understanding of myself as well as human nature in general. In undergraduate school, I pursued the study and received degrees in both psychology and religion. I was trying to find areas of science, philosophy, and psychology that strived to comprehend the interconnectedness of diversity. I was interested in ways of thinking that facilitated inclusion and synthesis rather than further dissecting and analyzing differences. My interests led me to the study of ancient Eastern systems of conceptualizing and working with human suffering, including Buddhist, Hindu (Yoga), and more recently, the Jewish mystical tradition of the Kabbalah. The pursuit of acquiring Eastern knowledge facilitated my finding many teachers who have influenced me both personally and professionally. These teachers included Cynthia Pearce and Tom Forman, who were advanced students of G. I. Gurjieff, a Russian integrative thinker of Eastern and Western traditions. In addition, my studies took me to India as part of my undergraduate work in religious studies; teachers who profoundly influenced my own growth and who I studied with in India were Anagrike Munindra and S. N. Goenka, the former a Buddhist monk and the latter a Burmese meditation teacher. More recently, my teachers of Kabbalah who have influenced me have been Rabbis Zalman Schacter, Yitzchak Ginsburg, and David Zeller. During my searching, I studied esoteric ideas found in many religious teachings, and I became interested in the pursuit of how to integrate these ideas with working with personality development depicted in Western psychology. In 1976, I came across the work of Roberto Assagioli, an Italian-born psychiatrist who was one of the first to bring psychoanalysis to Italy in the early 1900s. Assagioli was a major integrator of ideas and developed a system that he called psychosynthesis. Psychosynthesis reflected the coordination of East/West concepts and practices. Assagioli was an inclusive thinker of his time and he saw the limitations of studying "depth psychology" that only focused on what he called the "lower unconscious," which repressed the sexual and aggressive instincts. He recognized the need to develop a "height psychology" to help liberate the repression of the sublime. Some people think that Assagioli's ideas were too advanced in terms of gaining wide acceptance at the time he lived; however, he is currently gaining greater prominence in diverse professional circles. Since 1976, I have studied with many students of Assagioli and psychosynthesis, including Tom Yeomans, Steven Kull, Lenore Lefer, Martha Crampton, Edith Stauffer, Vernon Van Dereit, and Vivian King.

Many of the Eastern teachings focused on a holistic approach to working with individuals' internal processes. As a young psychologist, I was faced with dealing with harsh outer realities in working with lower socioeconomic families in the inner city of Philadelphia. Early in my professional development I gravitated to studying both humanistic psychology and family systems work. The family systems view fit congruently with Eastern ideas since it also emphasized the study of circular processes and the interconnectedness of parts that regulated a system.

I have had many teachers of family therapy who inspired and trained me. Early on in my training in 1976, Steven Greenstein and later Bill Silvers from the Philadelphia Child Guidance Clinic were teachers and supervisors of my work in Structural Family Therapy. Later, I studied at the Philadelphia Family Institute where Jack Friedman became a close colleague, friend, and mentor of mine. Another dear colleague, mentor, and friend, James L. Framo, has also greatly influenced my way of thinking and how I work in therapy. In 1987-1988, I was acting director of the marriage and family graduate program at the United States International University in San Diego. I hired distinguished faculty and had the opportunity to work and/or co-teach classes with Maurizio Andolfi, Ivan Boszormenyi-Nagy, Carl Whitaker, Norman and Betty Paul, Israel Charney, and Virginia Satir. All of these people have had considerable impact on my work in integrative efforts. Lastly, I want to acknowledge my older brother, Mark Kramer, who is a psychiatrist and life-long student in Eastern traditions. In my late teenage years he introduced me into profound areas of esoteric psychologies that strived for greater meaning and purpose in life.

This volume is a culmination of work that has evolved over the last several years on the integration of healing inner and outer relationship systems. Part of this work culminated in a five-week class that was planned for one and a half years with Virginia Satir. Virginia is one of the pioneers of family therapy. She and I co-taught a course entitled "Healing Relationships Through Conscious Change" in the last part of January and February 1988. She agreed to co-author a book with me based on this class with the purpose of integrating the theme of spirituality and family systems work. (Unfortunately, Virginia passed on in September of 1988, and was not able to finish this project with me. However, this volume reflects many of her ideas.) Besides teaching this class together, she and I had many long talks on the topic of spirituality and psychotherapy that were videotaped and audiotaped. Satir, especially toward the end of her life, was extremely interested in exploring family systems concepts in the greater-larger-social context. Her concerns were to bring more peace within, between, and among people from diverse cultures. Lori Gordon (1991, personal communication), a good friend and colleague of Virginia's, said that including the spiritual dimension, one could add the dimension of healing work that included peace beyond. Some considered Satir a healer who transcended any one psychotherapeutic school of thinking.

This book emphasizes the integration of the principles of psychosynthesis with family systems work. It is interesting to note that Virginia Satir spent time with Roberto Assagioli a couple of years before he died in 1974. Satir recollected her meetings with Assagioli, who read her book *Peoplemaking*. Assagioli was very impressed with Satir's work, especially with her famous stances that she depicted as the blamer, placater, computer, and distractor roles that people identified within the family system. These stances very much reflected Assagioli's notion of subpersonalities, which were the diverse parts of the inner psyche. Assagioli thought that much of Satir's work reflected the principles of psychosynthesis. He conveyed to her that he would have liked Satir to make more explicit the spiritual dimensions that were implicitly embedded in her work. In addition, much of Satir's emphasis on the integration of people's internal parts and family reconstruction often utilized meditation and guided imagery procedures that were also part of Assagioli's work. Assagioli was very interested in psychosynthesis moving beyond the study of the individual to incorporate groups, couples, and families.

This volume reflects the wish of Assagioli to make much of Satir's covert interest in spiritual work overt. Toward that aim, many verbatim quotes and sections of the classes that Virginia and I co-taught will be utilized. The entire class, as well as my own collaboration with Virginia, were totally transcribed as part of a class project to help facilitate the unity of this book. Many students in the class helped work on the original transcription of the class.

There is a growing interest in alternative medicine approaches which is indicated by such evolutions as a department set up through the National Institute for Health for researching what is currently termed Mind-Body Phenomena. These include the study of the effects of meditation, guided imagery, and alternative approaches to understanding the body that have been influenced by ancient doctrines of Eastern knowledge that include spiritual teachings. Throughout this volume, the reader will encounter the integration of the above methods with focus on the interaction between close intimates. I am calling this new psychotherapy integration *Mind-Body Systems Therapy.*

Before reading this book, I would like for a moment to ask the readers to detach themselves from their usual modes of thinking and be open to possible new avenues of conceptualizing and integrating an individual/systemic model of psychotherapy. Words such as healing or spirituality sometimes conjure up negative images based on either personal experiences or the general criticism of an area that is hard to conceptually grasp since it involves right-brain, intuitive processes.

Sheldon Z. Kramer, PhD
San Diego, CA

I am the great sun, but you do not see me.
I am your husband, but you turn away.
I am the captive, but you do not free me.
I am the captain you will not obey.

I am the truth, but you will not believe me.
I am the city, where you will not stay.
I am your wife, your child, but you will leave me.
I am that god to whom you will not pray.

I am your counsel, but you do not hear me.
I am the lover whom you will betray.
I am the victor, but you do not cheer me.
I am the holy dove whom you will slay.

I am your life, but if you will not name me,
Seal up your soul with tears, and never blame me.

–Charles Causley

Chapter 1

Introduction

Reflections on Healing and Spirituality: Conversations with Virginia Satir

I wish that Virginia could have written the introduction to this book. However, since she is not able to manifest words in physical form, I offer to the reader brief, verbatim excerpts from a class we co-taught together in 1988 followed by an intimate dialogue that she and I engaged in at my home on the topic of this book. May her words help you to capture her "spirit."[1]

So one of the hopes that I have is that you will be able to look at any small piece and see the w-h-o-l-e. You were all introduced to holography. Any single cell of you contains your whole pattern and by that same definition every one of us contains the whole world. So that we can begin to zero in on that. And I suppose if there was anything that contributes to my being able to work deeply it is that process of being able to take the little thing over here and being able to see the whole.

Are you convinced that you had nothing to do with making yourself? You're not convinced. Are you convinced that your mother and father made you? You're not convinced. I'm glad of that. Are you convinced that life was never made by human beings and always was? And therefore all we're ever doing is activating life. So the next time your mother tells you of all she suffered just remind her she only activated, she didn't create. I'm asking you these questions because I think these are basic. I know I did not create myself. I now am co-creating along with what I have. But I did not—I could not make myself.

That's all there in the egg and the sperm which is not created by human beings. And a lot of people try to go off in a super-structure without recognizing that–it's very easy for them. You see, all you did is you got activated by the two pieces that have to come together to make a human form–the egg and sperm. And therefore the basis of all of us is something that already is. When you get that, it's easier to be in touch with your spirituality, because that's where you come from. To me that's very exciting because then I have a fantasy of a huge cauldron, tub, reservoir, that covers the whole earth and that is life–everything just being recycled.

I had a wonderful nun in one of my networks. She was always finding fault with herself. She was bad at this and she was bad at that and, one day, I said to her, "Do you believe that the Creator made everything He did in His own image?" She said, "Sure." I said, "How dare you criticize anyone?" "Oh," she said, "I never thought about it like that." And, she stopped. So, we're all manifestations of life, worthy of respect and love, and we're all moved by the same thing.

So, anyway, at this point in time, being a human being is a manifestation of life and that makes us all equal in value because there is nobody that can buy it any other way except the regular way. So the things that belong to any one person belong to everybody–the fears, the hopes, the joys, the wishes–and that's a big thing because so many of us were raised with the idea that we were better than someone or less than someone else. And the idea was to get on top so everybody else could be on the bottom. It's the same kind of principle that applies to religion. I do not equate religion with spirituality. I don't believe they are the same. They can be but I don't believe that they are. That's one of the reasons I could never belong to an organized church. That is also one of the reasons that I have many friends from all different churches and many people who I think are very spiritual. They range all the way from Buddhists, Catholics, Jewish, whatever, so there are a lot of things to take a look at.

The following are excerpts from a dialogue between Virginia and myself.

Kramer: Were you religious growing up?

Satir: Well, early I didn't want anything to do with religion. I did study some Christian Science, but I did that only until I got in touch with growth; through growth one experiences spirituality.

Kramer: What is spirituality to you?

Satir: The seeds for me are a manifestation of spirituality. And I knew life was something that I didn't make and nobody else made. Therefore, there had to be a higher power. Life was the result of the Higher Power and had nothing to do with the human mode. So religion was supposed to embrace this but I didn't see that in organized religion. So very early I remember taking God as life and nature as life. And I didn't have to go through all this hokeypokey stuff about doing this on this day and that on that day. This left me cold. For instance, how can we grow and be connected if a God up there is going to kill me if you don't do right? Didn't make any sense at all.

Kramer: For me, spirituality came alive through the practice of meditation. Through regular meditation practice there is a feeling of connectedness, a oneness and a vivacious energy state.

Satir: Yes, I think one of the hardest things is to recognize life as energy. And what we do to ourselves is we put up a wall and contain the energy in some way so it isn't free to move. And so all of these experiences have to do with flow. This is life flowing. In the flow of everything. What's interesting is spiritual teachers say don't hang on or attach yourself to anything.

Kramer: People think they can.

Satir: The problem is they are trying to hold something back they can't hold back. Life will not allow you to hold it back. If you try to hold it back it will reform into something that works against you. So one of the things to make it work is to let the life flow.

Kramer: That's energy flowing.

Satir: Life is energy. I don't see it's anything else, and it's an energy that permeates everything. I had a hard time understanding that for a long time.

Kramer: When working with systems that are very dysfunctional, how do you bring the spiritual dimension into therapy?

Satir: Keep in mind that whatever I tell you may have nothing to do with anything. For me that is the experience of people being with me–of people feeling connected–that's where it starts. Respect and reverence are the things you use. If you think the life force is fragile, healing won't take place. You have to respect life and if you love it you validate it and that's what brings about change. There is no cognitive way you can bring this in. You have to be it.

Kramer: You have to be in a certain state of consciousness.

Satir: You have to be what you are doing.

Kramer: You can't be a fake at it, you can't make believe.

Satir: No. And you either have that respect, that deep respect, what I call a reverence for life, or not. If you don't have that you cannot really make a spiritual connection, because there's nothing conceptual about spirituality. It's all feeling. All we can talk about is the effects. It's like the wind. You can only know the wind is there by its effects. You've got to know that the wind is.

Kramer: I think the key to reverence and respect is being extremely attentive and connected to the moment.

Satir: Yes, a total connectedness. There isn't anything else. I try to be totally present and leave behind everything else–accept what is in front of me. To me that's the only way you can connect. Being totally present, here right now with you.

Kramer: What effects do you think that this has on people you're working with in a healing context?

Satir: Through making contact with another person you allow people to take the risks and go into the unknown. Being present with someone you help them create faith and trust.

Kramer: I can see that in your work, creating a distinct environment by the use of yourself being present, being totally connected with somebody allows people's defenses to melt and they can be more open to what's going on inside.

Satir: That's what I believe.

Kramer: And things happen quicker.

Satir: Absolutely.

Kramer: In your work with people you utilize your hands. I see that's one way you make connection with people. Can you talk more explicitly about that–how you see that in relationship to healing and spirituality?

Satir: Let's go back to the energy concept. The use of my fingers is the outside of my skin. I also know there is a space outside of me that is filled with energy and that I can control that energy and that energy can move to another person so that the hand is a way of expending that energy and me with it activating it with the other person. Our hands contain the possibility of connecting with another person. It's like you carry your own jumper cables with you in your hands to connect with another life force. That person over there is filled with energy, but it isn't working, so you move in and the energy starts moving. The activation of that creates a movement which is healing in itself.

Kramer: Do you feel that's a lot of what happens in your work, this idea of energy transfer through touch?

Satir: Oh, yes, all the time. I don't always touch, no, but there are other things going on. The skins of many people have been abused, sexually or aggressively abused. I can tell when I take a hand who the person is. First of all, whether or not I can touch them, or if their hand is going to accept me. If it does, I can tell what's there. I can feel the tentativeness or the message to come closer. Like yesterday I said to a lady, "You are feeling cold." She said, "How do you know?" "I can feel it in your hand."

Kramer: Let me share with you something I experienced with you and a half dozen other people. It's the experience of feeling like your insides are vibrating and free. Certain people are at a certain state of consciousness whereby they transmit this kind of energy. I think it has to do with a state of resonance, when the energy inside of yourself is less attached to rules and you're really flexible. You can look at it from a physics standpoint. Energy resonates at different levels of vibration in our bodies. If a therapist is not role- or rule-bound, they have their energy at their disposal. Their consciousness is at a different place, and their state of vibration is at a faster rate.

Satir: You could go into a physics lab and reproduce it. There are machines now where you can take life and translate it into sound and color. Those are all vibrations. Every one of these vibrations is responded to by something on the outside. Rudolph Steiner at the

turn of the century was very clear there was music that could activate behaviors in the internal organs. If we think of the world as
total vibration that is activated by the life force, then everything is
reacting to everything else. Take a person who is hysterical. They
will pick up someone who is hysterical. The world is a vibrating
organ.

Kramer: Do you do anything consciously to help you activate your
energy or state of consciousness?

Satir: I can't say that I do, but one thing I know I always do is
check my own centering. Since I work totally in a world that is
networked and connected, it's always there. It's constant, so that
anything that comes up I can see it in this frame. The whole world is
made up of energy and I try to get a sense of wholeness within
myself and see what in the environment needs to feel this sense of
completeness. The whole world is made up of energy and all this
energy is geared toward growth. People behave in ways that don't
validate their life force. An example would be that you have a light
bulb that could put in 100 watts but you have a lamp that only
allows 20 of it to show. The 100 watts represents a totality. You are
showing 20 watts, there are actually 100 there. Eighty of them are
not showing, but 80 of them are not operating. Where is all that
energy going? The energy is going back on itself. My job is to help
their energy become mobile.

Kramer: You try to help a person establish wholeness inside.

Satir: Yes. A person has to work so hard to keep himself together,
because of that which is operating underground. As this comes to
light the light itself begins to work toward integrating and making
whole. For me that is the Higher Self. The Higher Self and the
whole Self are the same. When you are fragmented you are vulnerable to negative things. I used to draw a picture of the insides. I
would have a pipe and then a gap and I would have another pipe and
a gap, so that things were not completed. When the gaps were filled
in, things ran very smoothly. That is what I call the Higher Self in
operation. Everything is moving as one. That's a manifestation of
your spirituality, your self-worth.

Kramer: Any other thoughts about spirituality?

Satir: I want to tell you what I think. On one level I think it's
peculiar that everybody knows life wasn't created by them and

that's spirituality and how come they waited so long to learn about it. For me there's no question that nobody makes life and that's spirituality. When people say to me "What's spirituality?" I say to them, "It's obvious what it is." You can't create yourself, so that source that created you and that life is your spirituality.

NOTE

1. A full-length interview with Virginia Satir about her personal and professional development is in the Appendix.

Chapter 2

Healing Relationships

Healing is derived from the Anglo-Saxon words hal and holy, which mean to make whole or to restore to balance. When one is in a state of wholeness, there is an inner connectedness. This feeling of connectedness brings with it a sense of harmony, peace, and equanimity. The more we can experience healing moments, the more our lives have greater meaning and purpose. We have a stronger sense of inner congruence, which increases vitality and self-worth. When we are connected to a sense of wholeness within ourselves, our contact with the outside world is enhanced. Our perceptions are more vivid. We are able to receive more of the nuances in daily life with greater clarity. Life is experienced with more openness and simplicity. In this state of simplicity, we increase our presence to the moment and live more fully in the here and now. As we restore our sense of wholeness to our lives, we begin to honor and appreciate life. There is a feeling of self-acceptance, which brings with it a feeling of caring and lovingness toward ourselves. As we experience a growing loving acceptance of ourselves, it is natural to share and express this love outwardly, which includes our relationships with others. With restoring wholeness to our lives, we are filled with more moments of joy. We find ourselves having more energy and an enhanced ability to flow with life's continuous changes.

In this state of wholeness where there is more love, joy, energy, connectedness, and congruence, we are highly "spirited." When we experience this spiritedness, life feels precious and we grow to respect, honor, and revere an ability to be conscious of the miracle of life. Thus when we are full of spirit, we are in touch with our spirituality. As we allow our spiritual nature to reveal itself, we are in a state of healing and wholeness.

Satir (1988), in her later work, emphasized that the most important step in growth was to experience wholeness and congruence.
This state of balance teaches one to be energized and aids in the
development of being more fully human. According to Satir, when
one experiences harmony, one has a sense of self-worth. In this
positive state of consciousness, one is in touch with their spirituality. Satir states:

> I think one of the hardest things is to recognize life as energy.
> We put up walls and contain the energy in some way so it isn't
> free to move. We have to learn how to flow with our inner
> energy . . . . The most powerful thing I think is growth. The
> organisms in the world are geared always constantly toward
> growth . . . . The seeds for me are a manifestation of spirituality.
> A plant wants to get its head out and then it wants to flower. It
> then wants to make fruit and then the fruit drops and it's always
> pushing. So if we keep that in mind that growth is the main
> push and healing is the means by which we take away the
> impediments that stop the feeling of growth and vitality . . . .
> When one is in touch with one's vitality, one experiences self
> worth. For me vitality and self-worth are all related to health.
> That is the manifestation of our spirituality . . . . When you talk
> about someone's spirit they always mean something positive . . .
> in touch with aliveness–the life force. So that spirituality is the
> practice of being spirited.

Stephen Levine (1987), in his profound work with the dying, has
added to our greater understanding of healing. He states:

> Healing is the growth that each person seeks. Healing is what
> happens when we come to our edge, to the unexplored territo-
> ry of mind and body, and take a single step beyond into the
> unknown, the space in which all growth occurs. Healing is
> discovery. It goes beyond life and death. Healing occurs not in
> tiny thoughts of who we think we are and what we know, but
> in the vast undefinable spaciousness of being–of what we
> essentially are–not whom we imagined we shall become.

Levine (1987) adds how opening to healing in the here and now
results in experiencing an inner sense of aliveness and vitality:

A healing moment is one in which the mind is not clinging to its passing show, not lost in the personal melodrama of its content, but tuned to the constant unfolding of the process in a moment of being fully alive, a moment of healing. Experiencing the vastness in which all floats for even a millisecond has the power to bring balance and harmony to the mind/body. Each moment of participating in the spaciousness of being deepens the context for healing. Each moment experienced directly releases the holding about our suffering. Insight accrues as wisdom. Mercy accrues as compassion. Healing accumulates from moment to moment when discomfort is met mindfully, open-heartedly, in the present where all that we seek is to be found . . . . (p. 32)

Many people who have been on the path of self-healing have worked on themselves alone or with therapists or counselors, clergy, or some other advisor. Many people have thought that the way to increase moments of healing was to isolate themselves from others, especially their most significant relationships with their spouses, children, lovers, grandparents, parents, siblings, colleagues, and friends. However, the main theme of this book is that we can restore wholeness in ourselves through our human relationships. In fact, when we are fully present in the moment with our most significant relationships in our lives, we have the opportunity to open our hearts to the deepest parts of ourselves where we can experience the highest, most profound qualities that a human being can be aware of in his/her lifetime, including our ability to be understanding, compassionate, loving, and forgiving.

Buber (1970) discusses how wholeness is experienced in the I-Thou relationship encounter:

The You encounters me by grace–it cannot be found by seeking. But that I speak the basic word to it is a deed of my whole being, is my essential deed.

The You encounters me, but I enter into a direct relationship to it . . . .

The basic word I-You can be spoken only with one's whole being. The concentration and fusion into a whole being can never be accomplished by me, can never be accomplished without me. I require a You to become; becoming I, I say You.

All actual life is encounter. (p. 62)

Buber (1970) also points out how the human act of relationship is one that is sacred. Through genuine encounters, one directly experiences living spirituality in relationship:

Spirit in its human manifestation is man's response to his You. Man speaks in many tongues—tongues of language, of art, of action, but the spirit is one; it is response to the You that appears from the mystery and address us from the mystery . . . .

Spirit is not in the I but *between* I and you. It is not like the blood that circulates in you but like the air in which you breathe. Man lives in the spirit when he is able to respond to his You. He is able to do that when he enters into this relation with his whole being. It is solely by virtue of his power to relate that man is able to live in the spirit. (p. 89)

Buber (1970) adds that human beings have the opportunity through every relational act to honor that which is sacred:

In every sphere, in every relational act, through everything that becomes present to us, we gaze toward the train of the eternal You; in each we perceive a breath of it; in every You we address the eternal You, in every sphere according to its manner. All spheres are included in it while it is included in none. (p. 150)

When a man loves a woman so that her life is present in his own, the You of her eyes allows him to gaze into a ray of the eternal You . . . . (p. 154)

When we start to think of incorporating a healing psychology into our thinking, we need to find ways to bridge and integrate the individual's internal experiences with his external relationships. We need to utilize a variety of methods and procedures as well as ways of being with ourselves and others to enhance deeper connections in relationships.

Schools of psychotherapy have been warring with each other for years about the "right" way of conceptualizing and working with persons who are in need of healing. However, there is an ever-growing interest in finding ways to coordinate and integrate, when appropriate, seemingly diverse psychotherapeutic paradigms. In fact, many theorists and therapists believe that the next century will call on each of us to find this integration both in our work as well as our own personal lives.

Virginia Satir (1988) reflects on her vision of the future human being and psychotherapy:

> We have yet to see what the flowering of the human being can be like and now is the time. We are twelve years to the year 2000. The next century is very important–a century where human beings will be looked at in terms of who they really are. We've been preparing for that since World War II. We are in a place that no human beings have ever been in the history of mankind. That's what's so exciting about all of this. And it's all over the world. So we're children of the transition period . . . .

Satir adds:

> One of the hopes I have is that people will learn to love themselves . . . and that we would learn to grow and we would all be teachers; we would become teachers of how to become more fully human and we would look at the learning model as the model of change and that we could expand our abilities to see the many diverse ways in which human beings adapt instead of comparing and criticizing each others method to bring about change. (Personal communication)

One of the major divisions in the variety of schools of psychotherapy has been between the individual and family systems approaches. The major contribution of the systemic point of view, over the last 35-40 years, was to show that individual symptoms were embedded in a social context and that by working with the whole family, one was able to change around the interactions that were helping create and maintain a presenting problem as well as reorganize the system to continue to operate in better harmony.

As the family systems paradigm blossomed there were a variety of schools within the systemic approach that were at odds with one another in terms of how much emphasis was placed on the individual versus the system. However, at the very beginning of the family therapy movement there seemed to be a recognition of the need to bridge the world of the individual with the family.

Framo (1970) discussed the need for a theoretical integrative model that focuses on the relationship between the intrapsychic and the transactional family systems. Framo (1982) states that the creative leap to the family systems approach was recognizing the interlocking, multi-personal system whereby each family member carries part of the motivations and psychology of another person; they collusively carry psychic functions for each other (p. 39).

However, over the years, many family therapists have totally ignored, discounted, or downplayed the internal processes of the individual. It's as if the external system became reified and viewed as the only "true" reality of understanding the human dilemma. How is it possible to really ignore the individual? Virginia Satir (1988) asks:

> Did you ever think that there ain't no such thing as a family system?

Satir states:

> There is nothing but an individual in the world . . . there isn't anything else . . . . It's logical. If I'm the only one to open my mouth, how can I neglect opening my mouth? (Personal communication)

Satir adds:

> A family system is a construct to talk about a way of relatedness which is made up of actions, reactions, and interactions and each individual is a choice maker of what happens and that's in contrast to the linear model where there's only a simple case of cause and effect. The difference is–and I like to make this very clear–the difference is you take a microscope and you watch cells as they move about and you don't say, "that one is to blame for this." You watch as this moves and that moves and you describe the action, reaction and interac-

tion. That is a definition of a system. To work in a systems frame, you can't work with blame–you work with how things are attained, repelled, and ritualized. That's a systems concept–and that means that every individual plays a very important role. Then these individuals hold something in common. This something is rules they have in common which will determine what people do with these interactions . . . people need to know that the strength and the chains in the system is related to each individual person being able to stand on their own feet and be a decision maker so that they are not giving up their power. (Personal communication)

Individually oriented therapists often find themselves on the other extreme of ignoring or not emphasizing the ongoing real relationships with significant others in their patients' lives. This is especially true in the dynamically oriented therapies. Framo (1970) comments on how psychoanalytically oriented therapists focus off of the patient's interactions with others:

. . . One gets the curious feeling in reading the psychoanalytic literature that the patient lives in a vacuum, that the intrapsychic world is pretty much of a closed system and the environment is largely treated as a constant. (p. 9, *Symptoms from a Family Transactional Viewpoint*, 1970)

It is also surprising that individual, humanistically oriented therapists have also not attended to the world of real significant human relationships, especially the family. In the 1960s the human potential movement tended to foster preoccupation with the self, which often led to considerable narcissism. Many humanistic therapists facilitated individuals' individuation often at the expense of destroying significant relationships.

In the sixties, people found it easier to cut themselves off from their most significant relationships with spouses, lovers, parents, siblings, friends, and colleagues rather than to struggle with restoring balance in their relationships. Many people who searched for growth and spirituality have been hurt interpersonally and it is not by accident that many of these people chose growth experiences that involved separation from others. Consequently, many people made a pseudo-individuation, yet were not able to withstand close intimate encounters, especially with their most current significant relationships as well as their family of origin.

The purpose of this book is to explore healing in context of our inner and outer relationship systems. Through shuttling between the internal world of the individual and his or her real external relationships with his or her most significant intimates, there is a possibility to experience the deepest, most profound connections within and between ourselves and others. Through struggling with becoming balanced from within and without, one has the opportunity to experience wholeness as part of his or her everyday life.

Chapter 3

The Humanistic/Spiritual Perspective: A Bridge to an Integrative Individual/ Systemic Healing Model

Wamboldt, Gurman, and Wamboldt (1985) discuss four quadrants that depict different schools of family therapy that one could research. (See Diagram 3.1, page 18.) It should be mentioned that there have been new developments in the field of family therapy, especially with the new narrative, constructivist, and strategic schools since this circumplex model was created ten years ago. However, I believe the basic overview of the schools of family therapy still has utility. The first quadrant represents behavioral interventions and psychoeducational approaches. These schools of thinking emphasized outer changes in one's behavior with emphasis on adjustment and support. Much focus was on fixing the individual or having others in the family cope better with a problematic family member. The second quadrant represents the structural and strategic models. These schools worked with changing the external transactional behaviors between family members. The third quadrant is labeled humanistic, including gestalt, symbolic experiential and Satirian family therapy. These schools of thinking emphasized the uniqueness of the individual's subjective internal experience, especially the person's affective life. In addition, the individual's experience was explored in their relationship to connections within their most significant intimate others. The last quadrant includes the psychodynamic marital and family therapy and multi-generational approaches. These schools reinforced the need to integrate historical patterns of family life with present-day functioning.

This model of viewing researchable family systems paradigms is set along two axes, each of which is on a continuum. The first axis centers on a continuum from those schools that tend to look at "accurate" reality and traditional epistemology to the opposite end of the continuum which placed emphasis on a systemic-evolving model. In other words, this continuum reflects the theoretical position of linear cause and effect thinking (A causes B) (accurate-traditional) to nonlinear or interconnected framework (systemic-evolving). The second axis focused on those schools of family therapy

DIAGRAM 3.1. Four Quadrants of Family Systems Schools

ACCURATE REALITY
TRADITIONAL EPISTEMOLOGY

IV

Integrative Marital-Family Therapy ○
(Gurman, 1981; Pinsol, 1983)
Psychodynamic-Eclectic Marital Therapy ○
(Sager, 1981)
Psychodynamic Family Therapy ○
(Bentovim, 1979; Dare, 1979)
Group-Analytic Therapy ○
(Skynner, 1981)
Contextual Family Therapy ○
(Boszormenyi-Nagy & Ulrich, 1981)
Family Systems Therapy ○
(Bowen, 1978)

I

○ Parent Management Training
(Patterson et al., 1982)

○ Behavioral Marital Therapy (Jacobs & Margolin, 1979)

○ Psychoeducational Treatments for Schizophrenia (Rohrbaugh, 1983)

○ McMaster Model Therapy (Epstein & Bishop, 1981)
○ Functional Family Therapy
(Barton & Alexander, 1981)

AESTHETIC_____PRAGMATIC

Client-Centered Therapy ○
(Levant, 1978)

Humanistic Family Therapy ○
(Satir, 1967)

Gestalt Family Therapy ○
(Kempler, 1974)

Symbolic-Experiential Family ○
Therapy
(Whitaker & Keith, 1981)

III

○ Mental Research Institute Brief Therapy (Fisch, Weakland, & Segal, 1982)

○ Strategic Family Therapy (Haley, 1976; Stanton, 1981)

○ Structural Family Therapy (Minuchin & Fishman, 1981)

○ Milan Systemic Therapy
(Palazzoli, Boscolo, Cecchin, & Prata, 1978)

II

EVOLVING REALITY
SYSTEMIC EPISTEMOLOGY

(From chapter on Integrating Research and Clinical Practice, Wamboldt, F., Gurman, A., and Wamboldt, M., from *Marital and Family Therapy Research: The Meaning for the Clinician*, The Family Therapy Collection, Aspen Pub., Rockville, MD.)

that reflected the aesthetic to those that were more pragmatically focused.

The aesthetic dimension focuses on values, meaning, and purpose in contrast to pragmatics that attend to concrete, measurable behavioral changes and a goal orientation. It was concluded that the quadrant that needed most investigation and research was of the humanistic school of family therapy.

Part of the difficulty in researching a humanistic family therapy is that the field of humanistic-existential psychology is not a remarkably cohesive group of ideas; instead it has reflected a broad movement and philosophy that spans many continents and embraces a large number of psychologists and psychiatrists, especially in Europe and America, who have called themselves humanists, phenomenologists, and existentialists.

Another problem of investigating and researching the humanistic position is that its basic constructs move toward the aesthetic realm where articulating concepts is difficult since many of the humanistic ideas come from inner experiences that are closer to processes that involve one's intuition.

The purpose of this chapter is to review the common threads of humanistic-existential thinking and look at them in relationship to formulating an integrative individual/systemic model of healing.

The basic humanistic psychological principle is one of the potential of an individual to grow. In addition, humanistic psychologists believe that there is something intrinsically good, beautiful, and aesthetic about the human being that makes him or her precious among all other living creatures. At the heart of humanistic philosophy is that the human being has the ability not to be a victim to the environment. Human beings have a degree of autonomy and some freedom to choose. From this point of view, humanistic psychotherapy evolved against a view of persons as machines confined by dualism, reductionism, and determinism. Humanistic thinkers have declared that the Newtonian-Cartesian paradigm is obsolete.

Other dimensions of humanistic psychology involve themes of focusing on the capacity for self-awareness and commitment in the face of uncertainty, finding one's unique identity and relating to others in a meaningful way, the courage to face one's aloneness for oneself, the search for meaning, values, purpose and goals, acceptance of existential anxiety, and the awareness of death and nonbeing.

When one focuses on these particular themes found within humanistic psychology and compares them with underlying principles found within family therapy, we find that there are pieces of these concepts that run through many of the schools of family therapy. Ivan Boszormenyi-Nagy's work in contextual family therapy focuses on issues of responsibility, commitment, and the search for values, purpose, and meaning within the family system. Carl Whitaker's work also encompasses some of these particular themes (Neil and Kniskern, 1982). Whitaker provokes families to look at existential issues which in turn aids the family in reflecting on itself so that it can choose another way of being that would be more harmonious. Norman and Betty Paul's work on the central importance of dealing with loss incorporates a humanistic/existential position. Israel Charney's (1992) work on existential-dialogical work also encompasses the humanistic perspective with family systems work.

Virginia Satir, the mother of family therapy, has brought the most influence of humanistic principles, including themes that include the capacity for self-awareness, working with affect, growth, and taking responsibility for oneself. Other family therapists who have utilized some of these constructs have included Kempler, who integrated Gestalt therapy in working with families, and Levant, who integrated Carl Rogers' client-centered concepts of working with families.

Part of the difficulty with integrating humanistic concepts with family therapy has to do with the struggles that family theorists and therapists have with epistemology. The original metaphor of the cybernetic machine holding the family to a presumed steady state has been a metaphor for the repetitive interaction loops seen in families with symptomatic family members. Hoffman (1981) describes it as the counterpart in family therapy to the idea of resistance in individual therapy. Thus the ideas of resistance or family homeostasis are closer to a linear position. Dell (1982) has challenged family systems concepts; he states, "The system does not resist, it only behaves in accordance with its own coherence." Dell talks of the need to shift from the homeostatic position to an evolutionary paradigm. From this point of view, a symptom, instead of being viewed as indicating a dysfunctional family, can be seen as a variable that keeps pushing the family to a new state. Dell (1982) in his article, "Beyond Homeostasis," states that there is a complementarity and coevolution that takes place among the behavioral coherences of the individuals and between them and the system as a whole. He addresses the issue that the behavioral coherence of each individual member has the potential for behaviors that can discontinuously transform the coherence of the system.

The idea of individual members of the system having the potential to transform the fit of others' position in the relationship system is closer to the heart of humanistic philosophy. One of the major themes in humanistic psychology is the universal assumption of the actualizing tendency or drive endemic to all living organisms. Many authors translate this into a drive or tendency toward actualization. It is an antihomeostatic concept in that it depicts the organism as constantly striving to actualize new potentialities as they develop during the course of life rather than merely seeking to maintain or restore the equilibrium. In other words, living organisms and systems do the best they can at all the stages of their development to actualize their potentialities at any point in time. This idea of living systems being in the process of becoming is related to the principle of syntropy, or negative entropy, which is the principle that forms tend to reach higher levels of organization, order, and dynamic harmony, and this stands in contrast to the classic principle found in science and entropy, which is the factor found within nature that causes organisms to disintegrate into lower levels of organization. Albert Szent-Gyoergyi (1974), research botanist, who has been twice awarded the Nobel Prize, describes the "innate drive of living matter to perfect itself" which suggests that the syntropic principle can be found even at the subatomic level of matter. By "drive" Szent-Gyoergyi simply means the ability of life to maintain and improve itself. Buckminster Fuller (1969), for example, states, "the history of man seems to demonstrate the emergence of this constant state of participation and theretofore spontaneous evolution." Szent-Gyoergyi says that there seems to exist a wisdom of the body, that is, the notion of living systems having a drive or tendency toward evolution or perfection.

The idea of growth, human potential, and the drive in living systems to become more complex and to evolve into systems that are more harmonious is part of humanistic psychology's third force position. In order to integrate these major constructs within one's thinking, the question would be: How do we help individuals and families tap into their own process of evolution?

There is a need for a coherent model to bridge humanistic concepts within an individual/systemic framework. Toward that aim, this chapter will introduce the work of Roberto Assagioli and his development of psychosynthesis which integrates the humanistic and spiritual dimensions of the person.

ROBERTO ASSAGIOLI AND PSYCHOSYNTHESIS: BRIDGING HUMANISM WITH SPIRITUALITY

Roberto Assagioli was born on February 27, 1888, in Venice, Italy. He lived in Venice until he went to medical school in Florence in 1906. Assagioli was beginning to publish articles on psychology and therapy in the early 1900s. He was working to find the common boundaries of medicine, education, and religion, which led him to the work he called "psychosynthesis."

Assagioli was clearly involved with psychoanalysis, and was in contact with Sigmund Freud. He was one of the first individuals who brought psychoanalysis to Italy via a professional article written in 1910. Assagioli trained with one of the early pioneers of psychiatry, Eugene Bleuler. Bleuler was the director of a large hospital in Zurich where Carl Jung (pioneer of transpersonal psychology, study of the relationship between psychology and religion) had also worked from 1900. Bleuler coined the word schizophrenia, which was defined as the "splitting of the mind" as it was perceived. This idea of the splitting of the mind later greatly affected Assagioli's work in psychosynthesis (see section that follows on subpersonalities).

Assagioli, in the very beginning of his contacts with Freud, saw the limitations of psychoanalytic thinking. He was more interested in creating a scientific psychology that included the whole person—creativity, will, joy, and wisdom, as well as the world of impulses and drives. His position was not that psychoanalysis was an incorrect approach, but rather that it was incomplete, as Freud had not given enough emphasis to the positive and inspirational aspects of the human.

Assagioli continued researching diverse areas of knowledge. Besides studying traditional psychoanalysis, he was involved with esoteric teachings. He was in contact with Rabidrinath Tagore (Indian inspirational writer/poet), Piryat Khan (a sufi leader) and was influenced by Steiner, Suzuki, and P. D. Ouspeusky (student of G. I. Gurjieff). He was very close with Alice Bailey, an English spiritual leader. In the 1920s and 1930s, Assagioli became good friends with Carl Jung, Kerserling, and Buber.

Although Assagioli spent a great deal of time developing his model of synthesis with the individual, he was very interested in the integration between the individual and his social existence. He conceived of each human being as a cell of the human group and groups of cells formed associations with other cells which in turn formed complex associations, like organs in the body. Assagioli (1965b) states:

> . . . An isolated individual, is a nonexistent abstraction. In reality each individual is interwoven into an intricate network of vital, psychological, and spiritual relations involving mutual exchange and interactions with many other individuals. Each is included in, and forms a constituent part of, various human groups and groups of groups, in the same way a cell is a tiny part of an organ within a living organism. Therefore, individual psychosynthesis is only a step towards interindividual psychosynthesis.

Assagioli (1965b) adds:

> . . . All human individuals and groups of all kinds should be regarded as elements, cells, or organs (that is, living parts) of a greater organism which included the whole of mankind. Thus the principle of and the trend to synthesis carries us from group to group in ever-wider circles to humanity as an integral whole. The essential unity of origin of nature and aims and the unbreakable interdependence and solidarity between all human beings and groups are a spiritual, psychological and practical reality. It cannot be suppressed, however often it may be negated and violated through the numberless conflicts in

which men foolishly and painfully squander their precious energies and even deprive each other of the sacred gift of life.

Assagioli (1972) was interested in the synthesis of the couple and family; however, he did not write in any depth on this topic although he wanted psychosynthesis to be developed in the area of relationships. In a very short paper on the synthesis of couples, he states:

> Synthesis of the couple is immensely difficult. The interplay and communion of two individuals does not exist. Why? Because the individual as a unified being does not exist. But instead each person is a multiplicity of subpersonalities . . . therefore, a couple is an interplay of relationships between multiplicities . . . .

Assagioli (1965b) discussed the crisis of marital and family life:

> The first of such human groupings is that of a man and a woman, the couple. It is the smallest and the simplest from the *quantitative* standpoint, that is, considering the number of its component elements. But *qualitatively* it is one of the most complex, owing to the multiplicity and closeness not only of the mutual interactions, but also of the intimate physio-psycho-spiritual interpenetrations and fusions that occur in the man-woman relationship. This explains why it is so difficult for a spontaneous, almost automatic, psychosynthesis or harmonious relation and cooperation to happen, as people with a naive and disastrous ignorance of the complexities of human nature generally expect. Abundant evidence of this difficulty is provided by the almost universal conflicts and the frequent dramas that jeopardize and not infrequently break up the marriage relationship. Adequate psychological knowledge and understanding and a conscious use of the methods of psychosynthesis would effectively help humanity to avoid and to eliminate an incalculable amount of suffering.

> The second psychological group or entity is the family. In the past its members were closely knitted together, and it often exerted a limiting and coercive influence on them. At present

the family group is passing through a serious crisis, chiefly owing to accentuated differences, and consequent acute conflicts, between the older and the younger generations. The study and elimination of these conflicts and the establishing of harmonious and constructive relations between the members of the family group is an important part of psychosynthetic education. May we emphasize that this includes the education of the parents no less than the education of the sons and daughters.

It is interesting to note that Virginia Satir studied with Assagioli just prior to his death in 1974. In fact, Assagioli read Satir's book, *Peoplemaking*. He told Virginia that her work reflected the principles of psychosynthesis, especially in regard to Virginia's sculptured stances of the placater, blamer, distractor, and computer. This work certainly was congruent with Assagioli's notion of subpersonalities.

With the preceding section briefly reviewing the background of Roberto Assagioli, it is now time to ask what exactly is meant by the term psychosynthesis.

Psychosynthesis is a name for the natural process of personal growth. The psychosynthesis perspective views growth as a natural tendency in each of us to harmonize our various aspects at higher levels of organization. It is considered a process whereby each individual who chooses to participate in this evolution can cooperate with the natural process in living matter to perfect itself. Synthesis aims at facilitating this ongoing natural process. Psychosynthesis is a holistic psychotherapy aiming at developing all aspects of the individual. Psychosynthesis has unified both Eastern and Western philosophical and theoretical positions. Eastern disciplines have often emphasized spiritual development whereas Western approaches have usually focused on man's personality. The psychosynthesis paradigm views the person as having a unifying spiritual essence and believes that a human being can directly experience this unifying state of consciousness.

We will discuss this spiritual dimension in Chapter 5 in more depth.

Chapter 4

Inner Family of Subpersonalities

Now I would like you to think of yourself, with your many
faces, as a living mobile. Balance is what makes a mobile
work. The mobile is a metaphor for our many parts.

–Virginia Satir, *Your Many Faces*, 1978, p. 101

SUBPERSONALITIES

Assagioli was the earliest developer of the idea that we have
multiple selves. His notion of our inner diversity, as previously
stated, was influenced by his work under Bleuler, who coined the
term schizophrenia, which depicted the mind as divided. Assagioli
appeared to be also influenced by the work of William James and
his lectures that were made into a book entitled, *The Varieties of
Religious Experience*. James utilized the term, "the divided self."
James (1985) discussed the pre-Freudian view of diverse personali-
ties that was believed to be linked with heredity and one's ancestors
who were still haunting the individual and were preserved side-by-
side with each other in the individual's psyche.

Assagioli first articulated the notion of subpersonalities in a
monograph in 1933 entitled *Dynamic Psychology and Psychosynthesis*. He discussed how his close colleague and friend Carl Jung
was interested in the "subconscious selves."

In Assagioli's book entitled *Psychosynthesis*, he describes more
fully the notion of subpersonalities and the principles of working
with them. Assagioli (1965a) states: "We are dominated by everything with which ourself becomes identified" (p. 22). He goes on

and says, "We can dominate and control everything from which we disidentify." Assagioli stated that tied in with the concept of identification is the idea that each individual is made up of many identifications or "subpersonalities." However, always using the word "I" gives us the illusion that we are always the same person.

Assagioli's main concept connected with subpersonalities is the notion that we express different aspects of ourselves at different times. The aspect we might be expressing in one moment is not the same one that was there an hour ago. A simple way of stating this idea is that we play different roles in different circumstances. However, we often don't know who chooses the role we play. Sometimes a particular aspect of ourselves may be in conflict with other parts. Sometimes we get so lost or identified with a subpersonality that we mistake this one aspect as the whole of us. This can be very damaging to us as seen in extreme cases of borderline states of psychosis. This idea will be elaborated later. Each subpersonality attempts to fulfill its own aims, sometimes cooperating, but more often isolated or in a state of conflict.

A simple example may help to clear up the concept of our inner diversity. Many people cannot make promises to themselves. How many times do we find ourselves doing the opposite of what we originally set out to do. A person decides to get up early in the morning. One "*I*" or a group of "*Is*" or subpersonalities decide this. But getting up is the business of another "*I*" who entirely disagrees with the decision. The next morning, this part wins out and goes on sleeping.

Ouspensky (1949), a mathematician, relates an Eastern allegorical story that describes the human's inner diversity: "Man is compared to a house in which there is a multitude of servants, but no master and steward. The servants have all forgotten their duties; no one wants to do what he ought, everyone tries to be master, if only for a moment, and in this kind of disorder the house is threatened with grave danger."

Ouspensky (1950) discusses how we have multiple "*Is*." He states:

> First of all, what man must know is that he is not one; he is many. He has not one permanent and unchangeable "*I*" or

ego. He is always different. One moment he is one, another moment he is another, the third moment, he is a third, and so on, almost without an end. (p. 13)

Ouspensky elaborates on the concept of our multiplicity:

The illusion of unity or oneness is created in man first, by the sensation of one physical body, by his name, which in normal cases always remains the same, and third by a number of mechanical habits which are implanted in him by education or acquired by imitation. Having always the same physical sensations, hearing always the same name and noticing in himself the same habits and inclinations he had before, he believes himself to be always the same. (p. 13)

The idea that we are made up of a multitude of inner parts assumes that all human beings have this multiple psychological nature. All psychological difficulties can be viewed on a continuum from the inner parts being more or less associated with one another. The more the subpersonalities are split-off or disassociated from one another, the more severe the psychopathology (i.e., multiple personality disorder, borderline and schizophrenic states).

These rigid identifications or roles occur within certain social contexts. Different situations call out in each of us well-defined reactions and responses that are crystallized within ourselves. From this point of view, subpersonalities can be easily activated by environmental circumstances. It is often the task in psychotherapy to be able to become more aware of the situations in the environment that "hook" us into reactive, well-predicted patterns. From this point of view, a subpersonality is a synthesis of traits, complexes, and other psychological elements that are embedded in a social context. It is well known, after exploring subpersonalities from an individual growth model, many of the splits or conflicts between subpersonalities appear to be related to our internalized family of origin.

THE INNER FAMILY

As human beings, we all have been emotionally wounded. Being in a constantly changing external world leaves many of us with an inner sense of vulnerability. We all experience, from time to time, being afraid or insecure. We find ways to buffer ourselves from the pains of life. As young children, we needed to find a way to make our external worlds less confusing. We learned and developed ways to cope with inevitable frustrating experiences in our families. We gradually organize our internal world based on thousands upon thousands of early interactions with our most significant relationships in our environment. The idea of who we are as individuals begins to expand as our experience with others widens. We built up early images of ourselves in context with others. These early internal images we became attached to and identified with at a very early age.

The notion of the young child building internal representations of self and others has been well documented in psychodynamic object relations theory. Individual dynamically oriented thinkers have mainly focused on dyadic interactions mainly between the mother and child. However, the young child gathers many internal snapshots of his interactions with others including separate dyadic interactions with mother, father, each sibling, grandparent, and family pets. Other dyadic images are of the parents' interaction with each other. The child has an early picture of the parents' marriage. In addition, there are internal blueprints of our parents' interactions with their parents. Sometimes images of grandparents are formed without the child's real relationship with them. Images often get formed of others by the young child listening to his parents talk about others (i.e., grandparents) as well as through family photographs.

Early in our development, we also develop mental representations of triadic interactions including ourself in relationship to both our parents, siblings, grandparents, etc. All of these early interactions with others becomes our internal family system that is often governed by the original roles that we inherited from our family of origin. In other words, we have internalized our family structures which includes all of the family system dynamics that have been articulated by family therapists including images of relationships that are closer and distant from one another, enmeshed and disengaged, conflict avoidant versus conflict expressive, overprotective versus neglective, interpersonal styles as well as coalitions, triangulations, and detouring maneuvers.

The idea of an internal family world consisting of many images is not a new concept. Satir, as early as the 1950s, began to uncover the individual's divided nature. Satir (1978) discusses how our multiplicity of parts offers us untapped internal resources that can aid in our growth processes:

> Allow yourself to think in terms of all your parts, the ones with which you are very familiar, the ones with which you are not familiar, the ones which you have not developed and the ones which you may not know exist. Think of each of your parts as a resource, regardless of whether it is the same or different from everyone else's or whether you consider it good or bad. Whatever you have represents new possibilities for yourself . . . these different parts I am calling your many faces. (p. 12)

Framo (1982) also discussed the idea of multiple parts through integrating Fairbairn's object relations theory with the family systems model. Framo states:

> For Fairbairn, instinct is a function of the ego, pleasure is the incidental to the object seeking and aggression is a reaction to frustration when the sought after object denies satisfaction. When the parents' behavior is interpreted as rejection, desertion, or persecution, the child, unable to give up the external object or change it in outer reality, handles the frustration and disappointment by internalizing the loved-hated parent in order to master and control the object in the inner psychic world, where it is repressed and retained as an introject, a psychological representative. (p. 25)

Framo's description of this inner psychic world is closely related to the notion of subpersonalities.

> It is the emotional relationship between the self and some external figure which is internalized, not feelings as such, moreover, these internals are not just fantasies but become sub-identities and part of the structure of the personality. (p. 26)

Ahsen (1972) developed a comprehensive system of what he called the Eidetic Parents Test and Analysis which concentrates on internal imaging phenomena and how the individual relates to them. He describes the internal images of the parent-parent, father-child, mother-child interaction and reconstructs the earliest experience with the family of origin through eidetics.

More recently Kramer (1988) has developed an integrative individual/systems model incorporating psychosynthesis subpersonality work with a family systems approach. Caveney (1988), in her work with healing the wounds of adults abused as children, incorporated the utilization of psychosynthesis and healing the inner family. Schwartz (1988) has begun to integrate family systems concepts with the idea of subpersonalities. He calls the work the "Internal Family Systems Model."

DEVELOPMENT OF SUBPERSONALITIES: INTRASYSTEMIC DYNAMICS

In order to understand how subpersonalities are formed, it is helpful to study familial transactional processes. Familial transactional viewpoints introduced the idea that all events are considered as occurring within a configuration of transactional fields. Frank (1957) in Framo (1982) expounded that

> . . . we think in terms of circular, reciprocal relations and feedbacks with positive and negative, through which the component members of the field participate and thereby create the field of the whole, which in turn regulates the patterns through the individual's activities. (p. 22)

Satir (1988, personal communication), as early as the beginning of the 1950s, started to uncover the multiplicity of selves or parts within the individual. She learned this when she started to work with her very first family. Satir discovered that the internal parts we are made up of consist of rules that we learned in our families. Eventually, conflicted messages resulted in internally splitting off these experiences, which formed a variety of roles that different members manifested. She recounts her recollections of the first family she saw in therapy:

One day . . . this young woman called and said she wanted to come and see me. She was an ambulatory schizophrenic and she'd been seen by some of the greatest names in Chicago . . . and she said, "People tell me that you can help me." And I said, "I don't know, let's try" . . . and what happened was that after about six months, some nice things happened with her and then I get a call from her mother, threatening to sue me . . . for alienation of affections. And I thought I heard for the first time, two messages. I heard the threat in her words and the plea in her affect . . . that was the beginning of listening to the two messages in the communication and so I answered to the plea . . . ignored the threat and said, "Come on in; I'd like to meet you."

So that was the beginning of being conscious of what goes on in communication . . . so she came and everything fell apart . . . all I'd done with the girl and so I went back to my characteristic place and observed and I began to see that they had a cluing system that was different from what they were saying and so I watched the body movements and the different colors in their faces. I began to rebalance and I know now that what I was doing was extending to this woman a connection with me and helping her to feel less afraid and also helping her to say things she'd never said before . . . well, this took about three, four months . . . so she began to come in regularly. I began using what I saw there which I didn't have a name for, I got that later, which was the essence of the communication I teach . . . and I used this with other people . . . so I began to listen for the threat . . . because you see, I knew all about affect . . . the rest of the study is very important because in this one case I learned everything that I knew about family systems. So one day, I said to myself, "Does she have a father?" Well, of course, I knew she had a father . . . but men were not supposed to be a part of the emotional life of the family in 1951, nobody had ever thought of that. And so I asked about the father and according to my psychoanalytic teachers when I said to them I'd like to see him they were supposed to say "No, he won't come in," but they didn't do that, they said "Yes, we'd like to have him in." And so he came in and everything fell apart again . . . and so the second thing was that how the negatives in a family stay together and how the communication that extends itself to the double level messages. People are not telling the truth–not because they're liars, but because there is a separation between the "should" and what they are and that plays into the whole defense system. When the father came in, everything fell apart again and I began to be aware of the differences in the power, because the parents were the power. And what I saw was anytime the mother would direct something toward the daughter and the daughter would try to do something, especially in relation toward her father, then the mother would accuse the daughter of not doing what she said and the father would take the mother's side . . . that's a typical maneuver in schizophrenia . . . I saw lots of that and so now I'm into family process and how the power works and so we worked at this and we got it right and then one day I asked, "Do you have other kids?" "Yes," they said . . . this wonderful young man who is perfect in every way and so I asked if they would bring him in and they said "yes" and so he came in, sort of a cock-of-the-walk and when he came I saw in my mind all these people bowing to him. I said to them, "I want to make a picture of what I see," and so it was the beginning of my sculpting . . . so I put him on a chair, put the daughter down on her hands and knees and put the father over the daughter, looking up at the son, also trying to get the father looking up at the son and that was the beginning of sculpting and what I called manifesting what was present so we could see it . . . . So you see and understand it . . . and no one was doing a thing . . . I simply asked them what they felt like, to do that, and it turned out that the kid–he was a grown man, he was 29 years old–he had terrible problems, he had allergies and was nervous and all the rest of that, but he had to be the one who was looked at as perfect. I began to see . . . first I have a double level communication which can't be acknowledged. I also see the cluing system that activates the emotional life of the family and regulates the self-worth. I see the words that negate the family process with the power tactics. I've done all that within about nine months and every time, I'd see this again, I would try it and of course, the girl got better. (Personal communication)

Ackerman (1956) presented a conceptual model of interlocking pathology in the familial context. Ackerman was concerned with looking at the interchange of unconscious processes occurring between family members as they unfold in the interpersonal context. From this point of view, any single member's behavior could represent a reflection of possible confusion and distortion of boundaries between individuals within the family.

Framo (1970) also discussed the concept of interlocking pathology: he stated,

> Departing from the conventional, simplistic view of symptoms of intrapsychic entities and stemming from a central illness, it is the author's view that symptoms are formed, selected, faked, exchanged, maintained, and reduced as a function of the relationship context in which they are naturally embedded. (p. 127)

In psychosynthesis, subpersonalities can be thought of as internally organized patterns and/or types of behaviors which have been learned in terms of what significant others (i.e., parents) expected or demanded of us. Over time, these expectations from others can lead us to identify with what is being reflected back to us from significant others. Many times, an "irrational role assignment is the cause of symptom production" (Framo, 1970). Framo also states that the "implicit and explicit irrational assignment of roles in the family reflects unconscious attempts by parents to master, enact or externalize their intrapsychic conflicts about these powerful needs derived from relationship experiences in their family of origin."

To fully understand the process of irrational role assignment and how parents as well as other family members tend to project and distort one another, it is useful to focus on the work of Henry V. Dicks (1967). Dicks described Kline's and Fairbairn's object relations and integrated their concepts with marital pathology. Fairbairn's position is that unresolved ambivalent love-hate feelings toward parental figures become internalized in the young child when the parents (primary objects) become frustrating. The child resorts to an internal mechanism called "splitting." He splits his parents to fit a "good" or "bad" representational image. The child does this in order to deal with his dissatisfaction with not being able to receive instant gratification. In the child's psyche, he preserves the good parent image and controls the bad frustrating parents.

According to object relations theory, the child also resorts to splitting the bad parents into the exciting, rejecting and the ideal object. The exciting object is the seductive parent who excites but does not gratify. The rejective object actively denies satisfaction. The ideal object is the parent who is stripped of all negative attributes. This new idealized image is projected onto the real parents since the child must feel some stability. This three-objects split, according to Fairbairn, has a parallel effect on the ego. The exciting object responds to the libidinal ego; this ego craves closeness to the parents. This type of split, if occurring early in one's development, can result in an ego that remains very infantile. Because of the unmet dependency needs, the libidinal ego can withdraw and not show its vulnerability.

The rejecting object relates and reacts to the identification of the split-off anti-libidinal ego. The rejecting object is also viewed as a severe sadistic superego which persecutes the anti-libidinal ego. The internalization of the rejected object results in the anti-libidinal ego becoming fearful and guilty.

The other ego split corresponds with the idealized parents after the disturbed aspects of both objects in the ego become split and repressed.

The splits within the internal object world are closely related to Assagioli's concept of subpersonalities. For example, the "exciting object" could be labeled in the psychosynthesis framework as the "seductive one" or "the exhibitionist." The exciting object representation, as stated previously, is a seductive parental image that does not gratify. Corresponding self-representations to the exciting object representations could be related to subpersonalities that could be called "the deprived one," "the sad child," the "empty one," etc. The rejecting objects could represent subpersonalities that could be called "the critic," "the sadist," etc. The other corresponding self-representation to the rejecting object can result in subpersonalities that could be labeled "the frightened child," "the guilty one," "the suffering one," etc. The object split that corresponds to the idealized parents or self-representations will be discussed in relation to subparts of the ego ideal.

Tyson and Tyson (1982) discuss super-ego constituents functions and development. Their work can also be related to subpersonality theory. Super-ego constituents may be used as particular kinds of mental representations with which the ego seeks to identify. The representations include introjects which are models or representations of objects which carry the authority originally vested in the external objects as well as representatives of drives and of expected roles in relation to authority. The ego ideal is composed of subparts including the ideal object representations based on early impressions of parents who are perceived as perfect, admired, and omnipotent objects with whom the child compares himself. Another subpart of the ego is the ideal child (person) representations; this representation is the parents' image of the "model child" or person. In addition, there are ideal self-representations. The ideal self contains aspects of the ideally loved, admired, or feared objects, the "good," or "desired" child as reflected by others, and ideal states that the self previously experienced in reality or fantasy.

From a psychosynthetic subpersonality perspective, these ideal objects and self-representations are reflective of formations of subpersonalities that could include themes such as "the perfect one," "the ideal one," "the guru," "the mystical one," or "the devotee," "worshipper," "dependent one," etc.

Other subpersonalities not developed in object relations theory relate to the ego splits that correspond to the "good" self and other representatives. We carry around internal images of protective, nurturing, loving, helpful, grandparental, parental, and sibling representations, as well as corresponding safe, trusting, accepting, appreciative self-representations.

In order to further understand subpersonality formation from an object relations standpoint, it is best to understand how the young child deals with parents who are interpreted as rejecting, deserting, or persecuting. The child, unable to give up the external object, handles his intense frustration by introjecting the loved-hated object in order to master and control the object in the intrapsychic world. This introjected or psychological representation is at the heart of subpersonality formation. Good objects are retained while bad objects are split off and remain as unconscious "internal saboteurs" (Framo, 1970). The earlier in life splitting operations occur and the more suffering that occurred in the actual interpersonal sphere, the more dependence on the inner object world. The consequence of this state of affairs is that interpersonal relationships are distorted to meet preconceived psychological representations that are directly related to childhood disappointments and frustrations and split off self- and object representations. Furthermore, internal relationships are the arena where others are forced to change in relationship to others to fit in with a preconceived internal role that has once been internalized.

Framo (1970) widened Fairbairn's object relations theory to include dynamics within the family. Framo states, "the various children in the family come to represent the valued or feared expectations of the parents, based on parental introjects; sometimes the roles of the children are chosen for them even before they are born, such as in the case of the child who is conceived to 'save the marriage'" (p. 132). This process, as stated previously, has been referred to as "irrational role assignment" or "projective transference distortion." These preconceived role assignments help the parents deal with their inner object world, especially the negative self- and object relations which have been split off from consciousness. In addition, it helps serve the parents to preserve good self-object representations as well as remaining loyal in reality to one's family of origin. These fixed roles that are assigned in the family have a parallel relationship to subpersonality identity formations which help crystallize preconceived ideas of who we think we are. In fact, family members tend to label other members to help reinforce projections. For example, there are "black sheep," "bad seeds," "good children," etc.

SUBPERSONALITY CLUSTERS

Subpersonality identifications cluster together to form a variety of internalized familial maps that reflect dominant patterns in one's family of origin. For example, the controller (father), victim (mother), and rebel (child) or martyr (father), demanding (mother) and protector (child who is the defender of the father against the mother) or passive (father), passive (mother), and dejected (child) all could be part of one individual's inner familial subpart-world. One person could have, using the above example, splits/conflicts between three images of mother-victim, demanding, and passive; father-controller, martyr, and passive; and child-rebel, protector and dejected one.

All the variety of subparts of mother, father, child, siblings, and other significant early figures make up the inner family. When these subparts become crystallized and rigid they become imbalanced. The more imbalanced the internal subparts, the less flexible the individual can utilize the positive core of each subpart as a resource.

SUBPERSONALITIES AS RESOURCES

Before leaving the topic of intrasystemic dynamics of subpersonalities, one needs to understand that all the parts of the inner family are all potential resources to us. As described in object relations theory, there is a splitting off of "good" and "bad" images from our psyche. Utilizing the words "good" and "bad" or positive and negative are really distortions of the central core nature of subpersonalities. Subparts are always in their truest forms helping tools for us to use. However, subpersonalities can become rigidly identified with internally at the expense of other subpersonalities which we end up disowning. One part is gratified at the expense of others. This occurs in real family transactions where certain family members exploit or scapegoat others for their own sense of entitlement. At the center of each subpersonality is an energetic quality that is in a state of balance. For example, the critical part of ourselves can be viewed as negative; however, if our critic is not extreme in its identification, it has the ability for good judgment, discrimination, and discernment. A balanced parent needs to have the quality of helping a child better use his or her underdeveloped discriminative abilities. The internal frightened child can immobilize us, however, when we encounter its core quality, we can see that it has a great deal of sensitivity. This sensitivity can be extremely helpful to us in either positive or negative external situations. Even the positive qualities when rigidly identified with can lead to an imbalanced state of affairs. For example, when one is identified with the giving part of themselves, there can be a tendency to move to an extreme attachment to that external role. This can lead one to not allow themselves to receive, thus, there is an imbalance of this so-called "good split."

Satir's famous family stances of the blamer, placater, computer, and distractor when rigidified are dysfunctional; however, when the core positive qualities can be utilized the stances can be transformed into blamer as constructive judge, placater as receptivity, computer as a discriminator, and the distractor as a playful quality.

Satir (1988) describes that all parts have at the core of them a positive quality. She relates the distortions to one's belief systems:

> I start with a view that whatever we have done to our parts, they have survival significance, whether it's good or bad it doesn't matter. That's why it cannot be you over you, unless the Self is able to be free. I know some people, they're supposed to give all the time, so any kind of hope they have about receiving they have to ignore it. If you ignore that you increase the demand for the first part and you increase the hunger. To giving persons I don't talk about how you give all the time, I talk about how you receive–work out a balance. All parts are positive. When you release the negative of any part you are bound to find the positive underneath. So for instance people that are very punitive hide a quality of fairness. They feel a responsibility to make sure it is there and they believe that punishment is the way to learn. We have to remember a belief system is very important. What you perceive, what you believe has a very strong relationship to how you use your parts. (Personal communication)

The notion that all parts at their very core are positive resources relates to an all-inclusive higher center that exists within the self. This realm within the psyche is what Assagioli called the supraconscious (not to be confused with superego). The supraconscious will be discussed in the next chapter.

The main goal in subpersonality work is to become aware and accept each subpart as well as having them learn to balance themselves and cohere with other inner family configurations.

Chapter 5

Spiritual Dimension
in the Intrasystemic Context

We are all unique manifestations of life. We are divine in our origins . . . I believe we have a pipeline to universal intelligence and wisdom.

–Virginia Satir, *The New Peoplemaking,* p. 338

The topic of spirituality has been a neglected topic in the family systems literature. The word spirituality conjures up subjective definitions, feelings, beliefs, and experiences that are unique to each individual.

Psychotherapeutic healers need a common conceptual framework to begin to comprehend that there could be a realm within the center of any system that has tremendous power and wisdom to help aid in the healing process.

This chapter will begin to give the reader a conceptual framework for integrating the spiritual dimension into one's work.

IMPARTIAL CENTER

In order to integrate or synthesize subpersonalities, or inner family configurations there has to be a "center" around which this synthesis occurs. Each subpersonality has its own drive and purpose that strives to be expressed. The main therapeutic task is to contact a "higher order center" which is impartial to all the subpersonalities. This "center" can help to integrate and synthesize the different aspects of ourselves to make us more whole in our personality. From this "center" (also called "Personal I") we can act or choose what we feel is congruent with our emerging needs and purpose. An individual can learn to act rather than react. He can become more responsible (able to respond) in his actions, words, thoughts, and feelings. He can exercise this power of choice by the act of one's "will" which is connected to this "impartial center."

The "I" is a neutral aspect within the self and enables one to be more objective in observing oneself. In addition, the "I" or "center" has channels to "higher aspects of consciousness" which reflects our spiritual nature including experiencing qualities of understanding, compassion, love, will, and forgiveness.

The main key to understanding the "impartial center" is to reflect on the subjective experience that reflects its reality. When at "center," one is balanced and there is no purposive effort. When at center, there are no identifications except in simply attending to the here and now. To be at "center" is to be in an inner state of no action. However, it is a highly receptive, responsive, vivacious state. When at center, value judgments are shed since one does not need to protect oneself.

The "I" or center is not cognitive in the sense of grasping a concept or understanding a premise. It is an immediate, direct, intuitive knowing. The "I" is self-conscious, aware of itself, and in this awareness there is no duality. In normal consciousness, there are three parts, the aspect that is conscious, the thing I am conscious of, and consciousness itself. But in the experience of pure self-awareness, there is no object or content. There is no observer-observed duality. When fully experiencing the "I" or "center," persons remark how they experience it as paradoxical. It has been called "empty but full," "nothing but everything," "one moment but eternity."

The poem by T. S. Eliot (1943), "Burnt Norton," describes the permanent nature and the transcendence of duality of the "I" or "Center":

> As the still point of the turning world. Neither flesh nor fleshless; neither from nor towards; At the still point, there the dance is, but neither arrest nor movement. And do not call it

fantasy, where past and future are gathered. Neither movement from nor towards, neither ascent nor decline. Except for the point, the still point, there would be no dance, and there is only the dance.

Since experiencing the "center" is more of a *right brain* intuitive experience, is there any way of conceptualizing what exactly is this "impartial center?" Before defining this concept, it will be helpful to the reader to refer to Assagioli's "egg diagram" on page 44, Diagram 5.1, that will depict the view of the psyche. The lower unconscious (#1) is that portion of the psyche that is most analogous to the traditional Freudian notion of the unconscious, however, the emphasis here is on the primitive drives and urges. The middle unconscious (#2) is the inner region where various experiences are assimilated before coming into our conscious awareness. The higher unconscious or super-conscious (#3) is the region where we receive our "higher intuitions and inspirations." It is the source of higher qualities and feelings such as contemplation, love, humility, understanding, forgiveness, joy, ecstasy, etc. Our latent psychic and spiritual functions are in this portion of the psyche. The field of consciousness (#4) consists of the conscious parts of our personality of which we are directly aware. In this region, we are conscious of our sensations, images, thoughts, desires, feelings, and the impulses which we can observe. The collective unconscious (#7) is close to Jung's concept of the universality of archetypes. Notice that this construct is on the outside of the egg diagram, however, the outer line should be compared to a semipermeable membrane that permits a constant and active interchange with the whole body, as well as the outside world. Assagioli's conception of the collective unconscious is how human beings are so connected to one another and that "psychological osmosis" is going on all the time, both with other human beings and with the general outside environment (Assagioli, 1965a). The "Higher Self" (#6) is an autonomous function separate from other parts of the psyche. This region is not to be confused with the superego. Another name for the "Higher Self" is the "transpersonal self." The Higher Self is the focal point of the superconscious. It is a deeper and all-unifying-inclusive center of identity and of being where individuality and universality blend.

DIAGRAM 5.1. Assagioli's Egg Diagram of the Psyche (From Assagioli, R., *The Act of Will*, Penguin Books, Baltimore, MD, 1973).

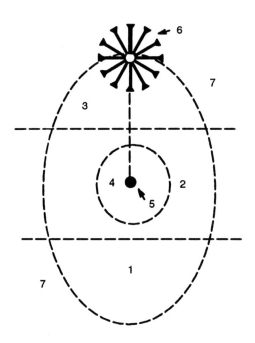

1. Lower Unconscious	5. Center (Personal "I")
2. Middle Unconscious	6. Higher Self
3. Superconscious (Higher Unconscious)	7. Collective Unconscious
4. Field of Consciousness	

The conscious self or "I" (#5) is the impartial center that was described previously. The personal self or "I"'s main function is consciousness and will (awareness and action through choice). This part of ourselves is able to truly observe. The "I" is not of the inner-family of subparts, rather, it transcends it. The personal "I" or self is connected to the superconscious. The Personal "I" or self is the center which can help contact the superconscious. The superconscious can send messages via bodily sensations, images, and thoughts to the personal "I" to help it integrate the subpersonalities. When the channels are not blocked, the superconscious is able to direct the person's psychological process. In this regard, by listening internally and through other techniques that will be mentioned later, one can come in contact with that part of ourselves that can help guide us. The personal self in conjunction with the Higher Self intuitively knows what needs to happen in our own process to help us achieve more balance and wholeness in our life. The task in healing is to be open to this realm in our consciousness in order for us to make choices that are connected to the individual's natural process that is unfolding. The therapist helps guide and facilitate the client's emerging process. The superconscious is the "wise" part of the organism. Through the personal "I" or self, the qualities of the Higher Self can make itself known to the client. The effective therapist will respect this natural process, and will better aid his client by paying attention to the emerging trends of the individual, by fostering and cooperating with those trends, rather than attempting to impose an external model of what the individual should become.

Satir (1988), in a down-to-earth manner, describes how the personal "I" or center is connected to her notion of self-worth. It is the moment in time when one can step back and see the totality of the fullness of all one's parts or subpersonalities. Satir states:

> Self-worth is looking at all my resources that are there for me to use whenever I want. I'm rich and look at all I got here. I've got my ability to be funny, my ability to be sad, my ability to act like a fool . . . I got all that and isn't that wonderful. And then my job is to use my parts in places that are appropriate. (Personal communication)

Satir (1988) discusses the importance of the relationship between self-worth (Assagioli's idea of personal "I") or "center" and the Higher Self when subpersonalities reach a level of integration, one is in touch with their internal wisdom or their spiritual connection. Satir states:

> The marriage between the Higher Self and self-worth is wisdom. . . . When I am connected with my Higher Self and my

self-worth, *I am wisdom*. My wisdom then allows me to use my parts in any way I want . . . . Wisdom is the connection with the universe. At that point in time, there is nothing that divides the self . . . . You can say that this self is the physical body, the physical temple, this right and left brain, cognitive and affective which are within alignment. Alignment is everything being together, the awareness of the body in harmony and in relation to the universe. That's why the relationship to nature is so important. (Personal communication)

Satir adds:

For me vitality, spirituality, Higher Self, self-worth are all related. We are made to be healthy. That is the manifestation of our spirituality. (Personal communication)

THE ACT OF WILL

A major function of the personal "I," self, or "center," as was stated previously is related to the concept of the will. Assagioli points out that the will has been quite neglected in modern psychology, psychotherapy, and in education. Part of the reason for this neglect has been misconceptions regarding the nature and purpose of the will function. Many people conceive the will to be a repressive agent that tries to "force" our urges and impulses into abeyance. In contrast to this concept is the will function as being able to help personality integration in a very "natural" manner without force. We discover the will through determined action. The will has a directive and regulatory function; it balances and constructively utilizes all activities and energies of the human being without repressing any of them (Assagioli, 1973).

There are many aspects and qualities of the will, however, it is not the purpose of this book to discuss these concepts fully. I recommend the reader to further explore these concepts in *The Act of Will* by Assagioli, 1973. In Chapter 9, I will discuss the stages and procedures of activating the will.

Satir (1988, personal communication) calls the ability to be centered from the "will" as related to one's capacity to take responsibility and make choices. She calls this quality self-leadership. She states:

> The person who is in charge of the leadership process has to know they don't have any support. The support has to come from the knowledge that their own centeredness and their ability to be congruent with people and their awareness with what's going on in themselves is what carries them.

COHERING THE INNER FAMILY

As one can establish this "impartial center," the goal is then to take this inner center of consciousness and will and unify the internal-subparts. Unification is at the heart of spirituality.

There are four main stages in this unifying process:

1. *Recognition.* The first stage in becoming aware that there is internal subparts that need to work toward greater integration.
2. *Acceptance.* The second stage is embracing different parts of our internal family to express themselves openly and honestly with their individual needs.
3. *Coordination.* Often subparts are limited not only by themselves but by being in conflict with other inner parts. In Stage Three, subparts explore with one another their central need and work toward cooperation.
4. *Coherence.* In Stage Four, two or more subparts work more cooperatively together. Through each subpart respecting and coordinating its own individual needs with each other eventually they are able to cohere toward a new unification.

In this last stage of coherence, each individual subpart reorganizes its individual needs and simultaneously compliments the needs of the other subparts as a whole. By creating a collective synergy there is a higher order unification that occurs producing greater strength and harmony.

Practical methods of working with meditation, body centers of consciousness and guided imagery will be explained in chapters that follow.

Chapter 6

Mind-Body Systems Therapy: Integrating Meditation with Healing Principles

There is currently a great deal of interest in alternative medicine and mind-body phenomena. In this chapter, I discuss the integration of coordinating and aligning the mental (mind) with the physical (body) processes in order to help individuals begin to bridge the same processes with their close intimates. When a therapist can track the subtle emerging sensations in the individual and collective bodies that are interacting closely with one another, one can see that there is a "relational body" that encompasses and transcends the sum total of the intimates. In fact, one can observe a mind-body dance between close relationships with complementarity and symmetrical patterns of breathing and rate of heartbeat. As partners or family members become deeply connected, their bodily processes also become attuned to one another. I am calling integrating the healing and transforming of relationship processes "Mind-Body Systems Therapy."

MIND-BODY SYSTEMS TOOLS

There are many methods to achieve the integration of mind-body connectedness with both individuals and their close intimates. The generic procedure involves an inner play between what can be called *disidentification* and *identification* processes.

The process of *disidentification* involves transformational tools that can help clients impartially observe themselves. This involves the ability to witness one's thoughts, feelings, and bodily sensations. In addition, one needs to separate oneself from subpersonalities and images of the inner family. This process is not to be confused with the defense mechanism of disassociation. Disidentification involves the ability to experience oneself fully, but from an observing position.

At other times in the healing endeavor, one needs to facilitate the client to become fully attached to whatever thoughts, emotions, sensations, or images the client is experiencing. This process is termed *identification*. The disidentification and identification processes are facilitated through the use of meditation, utilization of the breath, thoughts, sensations, and energy centers in the body.

Practicing meditation for both the psychotherapist and his client is a prerequisite for healing work. It is the apex of the beginning of spiritual work on oneself. As the client learns to effectively meditate, the inner work of healing is enhanced and the therapeutic sessions can be facilitated more deeply and quickly.

One method of standing back from the habitual reactions and working with cohering the inner family is through directly employing our mental processes. The next section will discuss the use of meditation through cognitive processes and the use of the will.

USE OF WILL

The process of meditating and "centering" has two functions: consciousness and will. Consciousness is a reciprocal function of passively increasing refined states of awareness. The will is that function that can motivate and put awareness into action. Activating the will is an active mental form of meditation. This form of meditation is directed thinking while in a contemplative state of consciousness. The following section will address the specific stages of procedures of mobilizing the will.

Mobilizing the Will

I now will briefly describe three main operations to mobilize the will: clarification, intentionality, and mobilization. These concepts and techniques will be integrated with clinical material later in this volume.

Clarification

The first strategy in mobilizing the will is to help the person become clearer on whatever issue he/she perceives needs to change. Before using any other facilitation techniques, one must get the client to see the purpose of working through this issue. The client must make a choice whether or not he truly wants to work on an issue that may be painful. The process involves aligning the person's "I" with the will to work. This can be facilitated through questions addressed to the client. For example, the therapist can ask the client: What changes do you need most in your life? What changes are naturally emerging for you? What is the next step for your growth?

Intentionality

The next strategy is to further align one's intention for movement into the future with the emerging needs of the client. If the client is accurately in touch with the natural next step in his growth, then his personal "I" will help to perpetuate the healing process.

One must get the client to see the purpose of his need to change. Once again, this can be facilitated through a series of questions. For example, the therapist can ask the client: What changes would take place in your life if the problem was ameliorated? Other questions one would ask the client are: How would you be different? Why do you want to experience wanting this change, and what value does this have for you? How can this change benefit you? All of these questions aim at clarifying one's values, purpose, and meaning of real issues in one's life in order to create further movement in the therapeutic process. This is especially helpful in overcoming one's resistance and negativity for progression in inner work. For example, a client who is experiencing a great deal of fear may be able, through the evoking of the intentionality of the will, to get in touch with how it would be to have courage. Painting a picture of an "ideal model" of how one would like to see oneself can help facilitate the will to begin to transmute the negative quality of fear.

Mobilization

If the client can clarify and align himself with his intentionality, the mobilization process will come into focus and be ready to proceed according to whatever needs to unfold in the client's process to help him/her become more whole. The main facilitative questions to ask during this last phase of working with the will is to ask the client: Since you are clear and see your intention and purpose for your next step in your growth, are you willing to move into the work needed to get there? If the client affirms he is able, he is ready to go further in working with guided imagery and inner family work.

For a further complete discussion of working with the will, the reader is encouraged to read Roberto Assagioli's work entitled *The Act of Will*. (See references.)

MEDITATION AND THE USE OF THE BODY

Meditation involves the conscious utilization of one's attention. The beginning phase involves the "centering" of one's attention on an internal or external anchor in order to become less distracted by thoughts and emotions as well as outside stimuli. It involves the slowing down of the sympathetic nervous system including a deep relaxation response. This process is not to be confused with classical hypnosis, although there are some similarities, especially in the newer, growing school of Eriksonian work. Meditation differs from classical hypnosis in that the patient is always consciously aware of his or her internal process, and the aim is not to move into a classical trance. (It should be noted that some schools of meditation, especially in classical yoga, do involve trance, or what is called absorptions. However, the type of meditation that I believe fits best in psychotherapeutic healing work does not have as its main aim the patient's attention being absorbed.)

The meditation practice that I find most useful is called Vipassana meditation. Vipassana means "insight" in the ancient Pali language of India. It is at the heart of Buddhist teachings. Vipassana meditation involves two main stages. The first stage is called anipani-sati, and it involves developing one's attention to concentrate on one point. One acquires this ability to concentrate on one point by focusing on one's breathing in and out through the nostrils. By practicing awareness of respiration, one becomes more acutely aware of the moment-to-moment process that goes on inside oneself.

The instructions to develop this kind of awareness and concentration are as follows:

> Focus on breathing in and out of your nose. . . . allow the air of the in-breath and out-breath to flow through your nostrils. . . . Feel the subtle sensations beneath the nose as your breath moves in and out. Let your mind rest on this one point. If you find yourself being distracted, blow a little harder through your nose and once again focus on the inhale and exhale of your breath through your nostrils.

Satir (1988) actively worked with the breath and often would educate people by describing to them the special function breathing has on our well-being. She states:

> Breath is what nurtures the body, and when you're tight you're only partly nurtured so the rest of you is hungry. The more tight you get, the more you feel others should feed you. Therefore, what you do is allow your body to be relaxed while breathing. You get a connection, an awareness of trigger points. The points are what triggers you to react internally as well as time to project parts of yourself onto others. (Personal communication)

The second state of Vipassana meditation is Vipassana-bhavano, which means the development of insight. The word "vipassana" actually means "seeing" to give insight into deeper understanding of one's mind-body process. There are different depths of achieving insight into the wisdom of the body. For the work in healing inner and outer relationships, the main purpose is to become more keenly aware of sensations that are arising and passing away from moment to moment in the body. Becoming aware of each moment in the body is related to what Fritz Perls, founder of Gestalt therapy, called the awareness continuum. In fact, Perls incorporated a great deal of Buddhist methodology in the development of Gestalt therapy.

The procedure to increase awareness is to utilize your attention to scan or sweep the sensations in your body from the top of your head gradually moving downward to the bottom of your feet and back again.

The directions are as follows (you always begin with the stage of Vipassana by simply focusing on the in and out breath through your nostrils):

> Allow yourself to focus your attention to the top of your head; feel the sensations on top of your head, experience them without judgment, maintaining an observing position . . . gradually move your attention to your forehead and the back of your head and once again just observe the sensations that are there . . . slowly move your attention to your cheeks, nose, and mouth (you gradually facilitate them, moving through the body)–through the neck, upper back, heart and middle back, stomach and lower back, rear end, genitals, legs, feet, toes. Once you reach the bottom of the feet, you give directions to sweep the attention slowly upwards through the balls of the feet, through the ankles, and moving to each part of the body in reverse through the top of the head. (When you reach the top of the head, you give a directive to return to breathing of the inhale and exhale of breath through the nose. It is important that one wants to be in an observing position when doing this exercise.)

It is often useful to have clients do this procedure in the office and also have them do it at home for at least one to two times per day for around ten to 15 minutes. By doing this work on their own, it will deepen the healing work in therapy.

As clients become more proficient at the utilization of their attention by concentrating on their breath as well as sweeping the sensations in their body, they can become aware of various places of tension and/or pain. As clients become more aware of the points of discomfort in their body, the therapist can help focus attention on these areas of the body and begin to probe through questions of what is being experienced. By having clients gently focus their attention on these points of emerging pains, emotional wounds often become encountered. As one continues to attend to and to move into the sensations of pain, one will often become aware of subpersonalities which need to be healed. The awareness of the subpersonality often begins the exploring of the inner family.

BODY CENTERS OF CONSCIOUSNESS

When working with transformational processes, especially in the body, utilizing a variety of meditation procedures, one will encounter expansion of energies that were previously stifled. In many esoteric and Eastern teachings, including Buddhist, Hindu, and Jewish (Kaballah) writings, there are mentions of centers of psychic energy that are located in the human body. The different systems do not all agree on the precise location of these centers in the body.

These centers existing in the body are connected to different states of consciousness as well as to stages of development. The renowned psychologist Abraham Maslow's hierarchy of needs fits here in understanding these different states of awareness and needs including physiological (hunger, sleep, sex), safety (stability, order, control), belonging and love (family, friendship), self-esteem (self-respect), and self-actualization (self-expression, creativity, experiencing of mystical and peak experiences).

In the Hindu (Yoga) system of dimensions of consciousness, there are seven centers (called chakras) existing in the body. Each chakra is associated with specific feelings and needs as well as with corresponding locations in the body (see Diagrams 6.1 and 6.2).

The first chakra, the muladhara, translated as root support, located in the perineum, is associated with survival and safety needs, as described earlier in Maslow's work. The main attachment at the stage of development is to the body. The focus in life is on ownership and possessions. Fear is the most experienced emotion with focus on the loss of physical and material comfort.

The second chakra is called svadhisthana (sex center), located in the genital area. Freudian psychoanalysis has mainly focused on the field of the study with attention placed on repression of sexual instincts and impulses.

Manipura, the third chakra, meaning the "fullness of jewels" corresponds to the need for culmination, including power, will, and control. In the body this center is located in the abdomen. In this center one fears domination by others, and feelings of inadequacy

DIAGRAM 6.1. The Seven Chakra Points—Front View (From Ponce, C., *Kabbalah*, Fourth Quest Publishing. Published by the Theosophical Publishing House, Wheaton, IL).

and being out of control. The attachment or identification is at a mental, self-focused level. One is motivated toward achievement, superiority, and status.

Alfred Adler's work has focused on the third chakra with emphasis on power. Virginia Satir's work on the will, self-esteem, and ability to have self-worth focused some of the time in this area of the body. In fact, Virginia would often place her hands between someone's navel and lower back area and have them breathe in and out of that place as she encouraged one to take risks. Many psychotherapeutic schools stop their work at this chakra as the individual is able to acquire enough ego integrity to have the person function and cope better in daily life.

The fourth chakra, anahata (heart center) is located in the chest area. In this realm of existence one starts to shed the need for

DIAGRAM 6.2. The Seven Chakra Points and Corresponding Autonomic Nerve Pathways (From C. W. Leadbeater, *The Chakras*, Wheaton, IL, Theosophical Publishing House, 1927, p. 40).

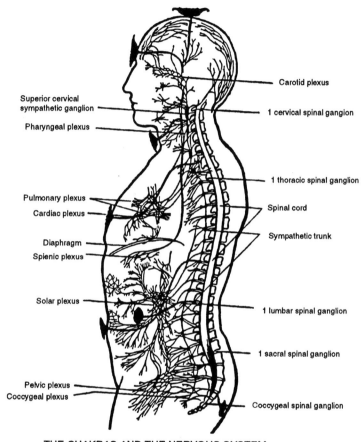

THE CHAKRAS AND THE NERVOUS SYSTEM

control, power, and competition, and there is a focus on the need for more cooperation, love, and appreciation for others. The heart center is a place where much healing work gets facilitated in relationship to others. The inner-connectedness between people begins to be realized with a focus more on significant others including family, community, or humanity as a whole.

In working with healing subpersonalities and the inner and outer family, profound openings in the chest occur where individuals begin to experience inner and outer connectedness and peace. One begins to experience "higher qualities" on a transactional plane, including a tremendous capacity for compassion, empathy, and love.

The heart center and its experience of compassion is one of the most important seats of transformational processes in the healing process. It is the ability to walk in another person's shoes and close the gaps of alienation and loneliness.

The fifth chakra is called vissudha (throat center located in the same place). This area is the center of the ability to be fully centered when one listens and expresses oneself. It is the area where we take responsibility in what we express, which often reflects our mental attitudes toward ourselves and others.

The sixth chakra, the ajna, located between the eyebrows and associated with the pineal gland, is the seat of intuition and inspiration where one begins to experience the unity and interconnectedness between all of life.

The seventh chakra, sahaswara, located on the top or crown of the head is considered the center where one profoundly experiences the realm of non-duality, complete wholeness, and unity. This center is connected to all spiritual inspirations.

In healing relationships explained in chapters that follow, one is able to begin to open and have glimpses and tastes of these expanded states of consciousness. One simultaneously works on integration of the subpersonalities in context of beginning to reorganize our various aspects around these higher centers. It should be noted that a great deal of inner work needs to be done under the guidance of a knowledgable teacher to continue to perpetuate the transformation of the fifth, sixth, and seventh chakras. This kind of development is usually best done outside of a traditional psychotherapeutic relationship, although one can begin this process through therapeutic healing work.

When working with healing family relationships, the therapist helps to focus individuals on emerging sensations in these centers that are always being perpetuated in the body and at times links these internal experiences with other family members' experiences.

In therapeutic healing work, much pain is contained within these centers that needs to be released. Many times, images spontaneously emerge, and one can express out from the image and center the pain that one has been holding and blocking. These procedures will be described later and demonstrated in clinical material.

MEDITATION AND GUIDED IMAGERY

The accessing of the subpersonalities through the use of meditation with guided imagery is a very powerful healing tool. Guided imagery utilizes spontaneous internal imagery triggered through bodily sensations, affective states, memories, or by structured exercises that the therapist facilitates. The latter will be discussed in Chapter 7.

The following steps are beginning procedures when integrating meditation with the use of imagery:

1. Have the client begin with closing the eyes, concentrating on the in and out breath through the nostrils.
2. The client is then asked to direct attention on emerging sensations throughout the body (as discussed previously).
3. The therapist can then ask: Is there any place in your body that you are aware of that feels in pain? (Sometimes pain is experienced as burning, anxiety, numbness, tingling, etc.). If the client positively identifies a place in the body that feels tense or painful, one can then have the client focus *full attention* on that part inside the body. Have the client experience the sensations in silence first. It is sometimes useful to have the client verbalize the *process of his bodily sensations.*
4. Have the client allow an image to emerge in the place where the body is in pain. For the person who has difficulty imaging, still with the eyes closed, have the client give the sensations a voice and express what the pain is like. This often allows images to emerge spontaneously. However, if no image appears, have the client continue to focus on the sensation and express in words what is being experienced.
5. The client is then instructed to continue to verbalize the sensations and/or image. If an image is in focus, have it described

fully in detail (this will be described later in clinical tran-
scripts). Instruct the client to fully identify with this *part* of
self. (The client is to imagine fully becoming this part.)

The above procedure is an extremely powerful way of beginning
to set the stage for working with integration of subpersonalities and
the inner family.

The use of the concentration meditation through the use of the
breath is the central fulcrum of being able to separate ourselves from
subpersonality identities. The use of the breath throughout the psychotherapeutic endeavor is the simplest and quickest way to facilitate the
work of healing. It allows the moment-to-moment exploring of the
internal wounds and letting go of subparts that protect us from experiencing the internal pain that needs to be accessed in order for healing
to occur. In addition, by the use of disidentifying from the internal
parts, through breathing, one begins to experience a profound self-
acceptance that further adds to one's integration.

Another more structured meditation technique that can be utilized is an ancient Hindu practice. One instructs the client to sit in a
comfortable position and relax the body through deep breathing. As
previously described, the following statements or affirmations
should be made:

> I have a body, but I am not my body. My body may feel
> different sensations–pain or pleasure, yet, I am not my body.
> The next affirmation is: I have emotions, but I am not my
> emotions. My emotions are diversified, instantly changing, yet I
> remain. The next step, one states: I have a mind, but I am not
> my mind. My mind is a valuable tool of discovery and expres-
> sion, and it is not the essence of my being. I have a mind, yet I
> am not my mind. After disidentifying yourself from the con-
> tents of consciousness, such as sensations and emotions, then
> recognize and affirm that you are a center of pure conscious-
> ness, a center of will. You say to yourself, "I am a center of
> pure self-consciousness, a center of will."

At this point, one needs to just allow one's body to fully "let go"
and to experience whatever happens inwardly (taken from *Psychosynthesis Journal,* Vol. I, 1975). The above affirmations can be

spoken outwardly or said inwardly. This exercise can be used with disidentifying from various subpart inner family clusters, i.e., I have an inner mother-victim subpart, but I am not this mother-victim. As one says these affirmations, one allows these images to emerge in his consciousness.

From the "I" position, as was stated previously, one can integrate the various subparts. The "I" not only helps direct one's process, it also can be fully experienced in its pure state. As has been described previously, the "I" is self-conscious, aware of itself, and in this awareness there is no duality. In our normal waking consciousness, our consciousness is directed toward some object either internally or externally. However, in pure self-awareness there is no observer-observed duality. This experience can be facilitated through this last disidentification exercise and with the use of other techniques found in more advanced meditative practices.

The pure experience of identification with the "personal center" can lead to awesome experiences of joy and unity, especially when the personal "I" ignites or draws into itself energy from the Super-Conscious or Higher Self.

WORKING WITH ARCHETYPAL SYMBOLS OF THE SUPERCONSCIOUS

The superconscious can be contacted by many types of disidentification exercises and meditational formats. However, there are other procedures to facilitate this realm, especially for practical purposes in working with subpersonalities. For example, when in the observing position one can contact the Higher Self through visualization and dialogue. One technique used is getting the client to visualize an archetypical image such as the face of a wise old man or woman. One can have other symbols emerge in one's consciousness such as the sun or a triangle, cross, or Star of David (six-pointed star). One then begins to dialogue with this image to help receive guidance from within.

The above images are usually vehicles for communication with the higher unconscious. Messages can be transmitted through other symbols or words. When using this technique, one has to learn how to discriminate the "higher message from one that emanates from a subpersonality," i.e., the superego as critic. At times it is useful to brainstorm all rational solutions to a problem and then proceed with this technique to help develop a creative solution that is in tune with one's purpose in that moment and general unfoldment of one's inner process. The exercise is as follows:

> Focus on your breathing. Focus on in and out breaths through your nose. Take a deep breath through your nose; hold it. Slowly exhale through your mouth. (Do three times.) Let a spontaneous image of a wise old person or symbol of wisdom emerge in your consciousness. Dialogue internally with this image about some issue in your life that needs more clarification and/or direction.

When a person allows himself or herself to move into the "center" of consciousness as has been explained above through a wide range of techniques, one is able to disidentify with the variety of subparts to which one normally is attached. When an individual can achieve this inner stillness, one can listen to emerging "real needs" toward inner coherence. When one listens to internal wisdom the person can move toward the next step in the growth process. At this point it is useful to further reinforce this state of consciousness by mobilizing the internal will as has been discussed previously.

MIND-BODY INTIMACY

The processes discussed above are mainly focused on the use of mind-body systems therapy with the individual, however, the pathways to relationship transformation involve the shuttling between the internal world of one individual and their close intimates. As this inner and outer maneuvering occurs both the individuals and collective relationship systems evolve. This process will be discussed in more detail in subsequent chapters.

Chapter 7

Healing the Inner Nuclear Family

This chapter as well as others that follow will focus on working psychotherapeutically with utilizing an integrative individual/systemic model. The therapist can work solely with an individual and engage in "intrasystemic" dynamics for the purpose of healing inner wounds. This process involves shuttling between parts of the inner family, however, if a couple or family is the main focus of treatment, then the therapist engages in shuttling between the inner world of one or more family members and bridges this work on an outer transactional dimension. As the transition is made between the inner experience of one or more family members to the interactional outer dynamics between them, the therapist helps the individual, couples, and/or families attain a new level of integration. When this transformation takes place, there is a new individual, couple, and/or family synthesis. The outcome of this work is that the new realignment of one's individual parts occurs in context to other family members' internal parts, thus a new coherence of the inner and outer dimension of experience is realized.

This chapter will specifically focus on different dimensions of working with healing the inner nuclear family constructions.

The emphasis of the work I will be describing is with adults either in couples or family counseling. These methods are especially useful when bringing adults together with their family of origin. However, there are implications in the use of this work with latency and adolescent children and their families. This will be discussed in later chapters.

METHODS OF HEALING THE INNER NUCLEAR FAMILY

Education

In order to smoothly facilitate inner family work it is especially important and useful to educate people you work with to what they can expect in intensive healing work. This kind of education can help build a stronger working alliance. Satir's model of the change process is very supportive and aids people to persevere through painful periods that are inevitable during healing work.

In Satir's model (1988) there are five stages of change. The first stage is status quo. She states:

> The status quo means I've learned how to predict what's going on and that's reliable. I can predict that if I do this then my mother will hit me on the head. Or, if I do this then my father will hit me and my mother will get mad at my father. This leads to a situation called familiarity. Familiarity is the basis for security for many people. The threat to the familiarity is going into the unknown, because if I go into the unknown I have no security and so in order to be secure I go back to what makes me secure. (Personal communication)

Stage 2 is the introduction of a foreign object:

> Stage 2 involves something new is entering this system which is in balance, predictable–for the purposes of change. The reaction of every system to the introduction of a foreign element is rejection. No matter how positively anybody is reacting to it. Rejecting. Why? Because it is unfamiliar. You will always have some level at which the organism is trying to reject. To encompass the foreign element you have to be willing to go into the unknown. One of the most difficult parts is to let yourself go into the unknown without support. But the support isn't, "I'll do it for you." The support is to allow you to learn to do for yourself. It is a wonderful experience for people but the person going with them–like I, if I am going to be the one to accompany somebody on a journey, which I've done many times, I need to be able to feel centered in myself. I don't attempt journeys with people unless I feel centered (Personal communication)

Stage 3 is called chaos. Satir remarks:

> The inevitable effect of a foreign element is chaos. Chaos has a physical, emotional, and intellectual face. Sometimes it has a

nutritional, transactional, spiritual, or contextual face as well. It means that everything is turned upside down. It is uncomfortable. It is intellectually confusing. It is emotionally disturbing. This is a place when this happens that people get headaches. If they have a tendency to break out in hives, they'll probably do it. I've had people faint–all kinds of things happen. Because what we're doing is we're lifting our feet out of concrete and we're in mid-air. This is the time when the vulnerability is highest. Vulnerability is high anxiety–and so people want to reduce the vulnerability by making a decision. They want to reduce the anxiety by cutting it out, however, you tell them this is a necessary stage for growth. (Personal communication)

Satir calls her next step practice. She states:

In this stage, you call for help. You have already learned that one can experience vulnerability without collapsing. The therapist encourages you to try out new behaviors that come from increasing your awareness of what has not been working in your life. It is not significantly different from relearning. For example, you help people remember positive images that come out of your work and encourage them to risk new behaviors. (Personal communication)

The fifth and last state is the new status quo:

At this point you are no longer in limbo. Your feet begin to touch the ground. The change for a new status quo puts the family into a new place. The change may be as simple as an individual can be more open about what they want in their family or the whole family is now more expressive. (Personal communication)

Another type of education that is also useful is to teach clients about the concept of the multiplicity of parts existing within each individual. In addition, one can discuss how we all get "hooked" and identified with a part of ourselves that others stimulate by their parts that they are attached to. The main thrust of teaching clients about their multiplicity of selves is to convey to them an attitude of not taking themselves too seriously. The next step is to teach them that there is a part of themselves that can be free from the reaction of the individual parts. The therapist can discuss how this part remains calm, objective, nonreactive, centered, and witnesses the activity of the other parts. It is also useful to have clients explore their "centers" by teaching them how to meditate.

This early introduction of the change process and some other general concepts of treatment is extremely useful and helps to pave the way for a smoother therapeutic encounter. Educating of the client supports him or her through the painful undertaking of accessing deep wounds that need to be encountered as part of the healing process.

WORKING WITH INTRASYSTEMIC DYNAMICS

As stated previously in Chapter 2, the repetitive systemic interactions that occurred early in our family of origin forms images that become inner blueprints that govern our current outer significant relationships with others. These inner interactional templates reflect patterns of boundaries such as coalitions, triangulation, and scapegoating configurations which can often be accessed easily. Contained within these systemic processes are subpersonality clusters that reflect roles that were rigidly identified with in the family of origin.

The goal of inner nuclear family work is to help the variety of subpersonality, inner role configurations come into harmony with each other. Suffering is related to overidentification or attachment to subpersonality formations. From this point of view, rigidity of identification results in narrow perceptions that govern our reality. The result is a lack of inner freedom from choosing alternative methods of thinking, feeling, perceiving, and corresponding actions in our interpersonal world. The goal of inner family work is to help individuals become more aware of the subpersonality cluster identifications and to help them disidentify from their various perceptions of their different subparts. As one becomes able to disidentify from the internal parts, the goal is to help the inner family reach a new level of cooperation whereby each part learns to respect the wants and needs of one another; this process is what I call "family synthesis." The ultimate goal is to be able to ultimately choose the inner qualities that one needs in the moment and for this action to be willful and not reactive.

ACCESSING THE INNER NUCLEAR FAMILY

One of Virginia Satir's gifts as a clinician was to work with her own images of what she saw in family interaction. She would then often have family members sculpt their positions and become aware of what they were feeling inside. From this kind of work, inner (subpersonality) and outer roles would emerge that could be addressed therapeutically. Toward the latter part of her life, she would work in large groups reconstructing their internal family maps via role play. Satir (personal communication, 1988) wanted to see these ideas and methods be applied in creative ways in working with individuals, couples, and families.

One of the most direct ways I have found of tapping into the Inner Nuclear Family is through meditation and guided imagery. Utilizing imagery is a direct way of accessing painful wounds that naturally emerge for healing. The following is an exercise I have found to be very useful for assessment as well as moving into direct healing work. (For a step-by-step guide to utilize the following exercise, see Appendix 2.)

> Close your eyes, focus your attention on the inhale and exhale of your breathing through your nose. Allow a spontaneous image of your family of origin to appear, including yourself in the house you grew up in and consider home. Where is everybody in the house? Is anybody talking with each other? Who is closest to whom? Is anybody alone or left out? What atmosphere surrounds this family? How do people interact with each other? Is anyone in conflict with each other? How are they dealing with this conflict? Who is in the most pain? Go closer to the person who is in the most pain. What do they look like? What is their body posture? What do they long for from others? If you experience any pain, allow that to be there and open yourself to experiencing it, see it as a gift to allow yourself to heal. Who is scared in this family? Go closer to those

who are afraid, see what they look like and what they need. Who needs more love in this family?

The above section should be guided slowly and at the end give a couple of minutes of complete silence as you tell your client to keep focusing on breathing. Then you continue guiding the client by utilizing the techniques that I call "inner family imaging dialogue." Sometimes the therapist intervenes directly with the images (i.e., by talking directly with the image) in order to help further coordination and synthesis. Other similar procedures are setting up a number of empty chairs so the client can shuttle between places that represent each inner family image and have an outer dialogue. The following can help to aid the facilitation:

Allow your inner family images to talk with each other. Do this completely inside yourself or verbalize the conversations quietly outwardly. Allow your inner family members, including yourself, to express their needs to each other. Let them talk from their heart.

From this above process, you ask the client what he/she is experiencing with his/her eyes open, which can lead into more detailed work with specific intra-system dynamics that need to be further worked with in therapy. Much of this work has to do with working with inner subsystems.

In the following sections I will give three common examples of working with the inner nuclear family. I will begin with guided imagery exercises followed by short clinical vignettes that will begin to demonstrate how to therapeutically intervene.

STRENGTHENING BOUNDARIES OF INNER CHILD IMAGE

The following is an exercise to begin to break up overinvolved family triads.

Close your eyes and allow yourself to focus on your inhale and exhale through your nose. Let go of any tension in your body and let a spontaneous image emerge of your mother, father, and yourself. What needs to change in the way these three people relate to each other? What needs to be expressed openly that has been avoided?

Clinical Vignette 1: Inner Parents Scapegoating Inner Child

Client: (named Betty) I see us sitting around the dinner table and my parents are unhappy. My father has a depressed look and my mother seems overburdened. I'm feeling scared because at any moment a fight can break out.

Therapist: What is happening now?

Client: My father starts yelling at my mother because she didn't cook what he wanted. My mother starts to cry. My father yells at my mother for crying. I go over to my mother and hug her. My father yells at me and tells me to sit down. My mother then tells me I'm not eating enough. My mother starts criticizing me for not finishing my meal. My father also starts criticizing me for not coming home on time.

Therapist: What needs to happen in this scene?

Client: My parents need to stop picking on me and deal with their own problems. I want to stop feeling so scared.

Therapist: Okay. Take a few deep breaths and go deeper into your inner child. Identify fully with her. Become your inner frightened child and express to your parents what you want them to hear.

Client: (as inner frightened child) "I'm scared of both of you." (Starts to cry.)

Therapist: What do you need from them?

Client: "I want you to stop picking on me" (voice gets quiet).

Therapist: What are you experiencing in your body right now?

Client: Tension in my stomach.

Therapist: Put your attention on your stomach and talk to your parents from this tension.

Client: "I'm angry with you. Stop picking on me." (Therapist encourages the client to say this statement louder and with more affect.) "Stop picking on me! Leave me alone. You're both unhappy. Don't blame me for your problems!"

Therapist: What are you experiencing now?

Client: Strength.

Therapist: Where in your body do you experience your strength?

Client: In my stomach.

Therapist: Put your attention in your navel area (chakra point). Breathe in and out of that point. What are you experiencing now?

Client: A sense of power and clarity.

Therapist: Get an image of this sense of power and clarity.

Client: I get an image of a tree planted firmly in the ground.

Therapist: Describe the tree to me. Allow yourself to become the tree. If it helps you can stand. Describe what it's like to be this tree.

Client: (Standing) I am big and strong. I have a separate space from other trees around me. I am confident. I have strength.

Therapist: (Encourages client to affirm the qualities of strength, power and confidence as the client focuses on image of tree and the navel area where strength is emanating. Client is also encouraged to image herself in this state of consciousness in front of her parents.) Go deep into this experience. What are you experiencing now?

Client: "I am strong and confident. I have power. I'm not going to allow you to pick on me."

The above exercise can also be used with coalition patterns where one child is aligning himself with one parent against the other.

STRENGTHENING INNER PARENTAL MARITAL IMAGES

The following is an exercise that ties into the inner parental image. It is followed by Clinical Vignette 2, which is an extension of the material from Clinical Vignette 1.

> Close your eyes and allow yourself to focus on your inhale and exhale of your breath through your nose. Let a spontaneous image emerge of your inner parents. What do they look like? What expressions do they have on their faces? What are each of them struggling with in their lives? What do they need from each other? Then let them enter into an internal dialogue expressing their wants and needs to each other. Allow feelings that have not been expressed to emerge. See if they can deal with differences without feeling unloved and unappreciated.

See if they can make different kinds of agreements so they both feel better.

Clinical Vignette 2

Client: I see my father being critical and angry and my mother has a worried, frightened look. I see her trying to please my father and nothing she does is good enough. She looks depressed, dejected, worn down. She looks like me with my husband–always taking care of him and not asking very much for myself.

Therapist: Allow them to express their needs to each other. Identify with each image of your parents–become the image and talk from that image.

Client: (As her mother named Rose to father named Ben) "Ben, I'm tired. I can't please you. I know you're depressed but I can't help you with that." (cries) "I need you to meet my needs. I want you to spend more time with me, help me with some of the housework." (Client as father) "Rose, I do plenty for you; you see how hard I work." (Client as mother) "Ben, I know you work hard, but I need you to listen to me." (Therapist tracked affect, which is anger, and encouraged it to be expressed.) (Client as mother) "Ben, I can't take it anymore. I know you work hard, but I want you to be affectionate with me." (In image–Ben turns away.)

Therapist: (Therapist talks directly to Ben, the inner father image of client.) "Ben, what are you experiencing when your wife talks to you this way?"

Client: (As Ben–inner father) "Trapped, she nags me all the time. Sometimes I just want to leave" (sad tone).

Therapist: (To Ben–client's inner father) "Tell your wife what you want from her."

Client: (As Rose, her inner mother, talks to Ben, her inner father) "I'm sorry you feel so pushed by me; it's hard to talk with you when you threaten to leave. I won't nag you if you listen to some of my needs. You also neglect Betty." (daughter–client) (Ben-inner father reacts in anger.) "What do you mean? I pay plenty of attention to her. I get on her back sometimes because she's not disciplined; you let her get away with everything."

Therapist: (To client's inner parents) "Wait, let's stop this. Leave your daughter out of this conversation. You're getting diverted. The main issue is you're both not listening closely to each other's needs." (To Rose–inner mother) "It sounds like you want your husband to spend more time with you and" (to Ben-inner father) "you want your wife to not be as demanding. Can you both work out a compromise so you don't go away from each other feeling misunderstood?"

Client: (Inner parents talk with each other) (Rose to Ben) "I'll stop nagging you if you can do a couple of things for me. I would like you to have dinner with the family at least a couple of times. Sundays I would like to make a family day–either with the two of us or at times with Betty." (Ben to Rose) "Okay, I will rearrange my schedule if you promise to be less critical of my work. You know I'm working on some very special projects that will ultimately benefit all of us." (Rose to Ben) "Okay, it's a deal." (They both smile and hug.)

After doing this work, Betty, the client, makes many connections to how her own marriage is repeating the same patterns as her parents' and how she uses her daughter as a weapon in her own marital struggle. She feels a definite inner relief from this work.

As I am working with these inner images, I could have identified each inner parental role (Satir's stances) as father as the blamer and mother as victim and continue to facilitate working with this pattern and trace it back through the generations. This would begin very intensive healing work on the "intragenerational" wounds that she carries around from both internal parental images. This process will be discussed later, in the next chapter.

STRENGTHENING THE INNER SIBLING SUBSYSTEM

In family systems theory, we know that when there are not clear boundaries between spousal, parental, and sibling roles of subsystems, that dysfunctional transactions can take place. As has been stated previously, these subsystemic configurations are embedded as blueprints of our inner family images. The following exercise and vignette is an example of working with our inner sibling images to help strengthen the bond between brothers and sisters.

Exercise: Close your eyes and focus on your inhale and exhale of your breath through your nose. Take a deep breath through your nose quickly and let it out through your mouth slowly (three times). Come back to your breathing through your nose. Let a spontaneous image form of you and your siblings without your parents in the house you grew up in that you call home. Where are you? What do you and your siblings look like? How old are all of you? What are you doing? Are you together or apart? What feelings do you have toward one another? Do you look up to one of your siblings? Are you jealous of each other? Are you friends? Do you play with each other? How do you play? What do these siblings want from each other? What are they secretly needing from one another? Does anything need to change in their relationship? Let them internally talk to each other about their relationship.

Clinical Vignette 3

Client: (Name Ken) I see my brother Bobby and me. I'm older than Bob. He's thirteen years old. I'm sixteen years old. Bobby is at the door of my bedroom calling me names. I tell him to leave me alone. He continues to make fun of me. I start calling him names back. I start hitting him and he calls for our mother.
Therapist: What's happening now?
Client: I hear my mother yelling up to me to stop it. I always get blamed.
Therapist: What do you want to say to your brother? Tell him.
Client: "Bobby, I feel like killing you. You always pick fights with me and then you get Mom to back you up."
Therapist: (Speaking to inner brother–Bobby) "Bobby, what's going on inside of you? What's going on between you and your brother?"
Client: (As brother Bobby) "Kenny always hits me" (starts to cry). "I'm just trying to play with him." (Inner Ken talks to brother Bob) "That's some way to play." (Bob speaks) "You never have any time for me anymore" (starts crying more). (Ken speaks) "I'm getting older. I don't want to hang out with you as much."
Therapist: (Talks with inner brother Bob) "What do you need from Ken? Tell him your needs."

Client: (As Bob to Ken) (Starts crying) "Ken, I admire you, you're strong and you have lots of friends. I'm scared. I'm being teased at school. I just want to talk with you and be with you more."

Therapist: (To brother Ken) "Did you ever know that your brother looked up to you?"

Client: (As Ken) (Cries) "No, I wish he would just tell me what his feelings are and not just tease me." (To Bob) "I'm sorry. I'll help you out if you quit calling me names and getting Mom involved, okay?" (Bob) "Okay."

The above simple sibling dialogue usually never happens in real life. Brothers and sisters have often never learned how to talk with each other directly and with mutual respect. These inner conversations can help to heal the inner wounds of sibling strife.

Chapter 8

Healing Intragenerational Wounds

I keep in mind the sin (actions) of the fathers for their descendants, to the third and fourth (generations). But for those who love Me and keep my commandments, I show love for thousands [of generations].

–Kaplan, A. , Yithro in Exodus, p. 196, *The Living Torah*

Intergenerational family therapists often work with three generations in one session accessing pains that have been accumulated throughout the life cycle. Many times, intergenerational therapists do not have actual access to the family of origin. Often the older generations cannot come into therapy because of long distance and financial considerations, illness, or death. However, we carry around subparts of ourselves that are directly linked to our ancestors (grandparents and great grandparents). These subparts images are often containers of a great deal of pain or wounds that we continue to perpetuate in our current lives.

Virginia Satir developed the principles of family reconstruction where she would work via role play with three generations to heal deeply embedded wounds. She would use large groups to do this kind of work. In the following sections, I have developed what I call "healing intragenerational wounds." Virginia wanted to see her concepts be applied in smaller contexts and she endorsed the idea of directly working with imagery to tap into these wounds. This will be explained in detail below.

The process of healing the intragenerational family is one of the most powerful and heart-rending works that can be experienced by the therapist and his client. One of the deepest connections with the inner family work comes through directly accessing the wounds that one generation passes down to the next generation throughout time. If one can experientially contact our deepest sufferings, fears, longings, hopes, and wishes and traces these patterns to our own personal lifeline with our parents and grandparents, we form a special link and bond to our ancestors. Opening our heart to our intragenerational connections leaves one filled with greater meaning and purpose in our lives. We have a profound understanding of our own link to the chains of time. When we choose to engage in healing these wounds, we release our ancestors and ourselves from the fetters of perpetuating deeply embedded patterns of suffering.

STAGES OF INTRAGENERATIONAL HEALING

The process of healing intragenerational wounds potentially involves seven stages. These stages can all occur in one therapy session or over a period of months, depending on the readiness to engage in the process. The stages of healing are as follows:

1. Opening the wound. The prerequisite to facilitating a healing process is having the client recognize that there is pain which manifests itself in mental attitude, emotionally, and/or physically in the body.

2. Embracing the wound. The next step is to accept the pain of one or more of the subpersonalities (inner family) that are alienated or in conflict with one another. This process involves letting go of the fear of other parts of the self that have been protective of the wounds. Traditionally, these inner protectors have been labeled as defense mechanisms that buffer the experience of painful affects. These defenses have been viewed as resistances which need to be dissolved. They are often viewed in a negative light (something that interferes with therapy). However, all parts need to be accepted (one can't get rid of any part). These subparts have acted as friends to us to help us survive through unbearable times. These parts need to be embraced and recognized for their past efforts. Through engaging in dialogue with these protective parts, they will eventually give room for other subparts that are wounded to express themselves. The protective parts need to know that they won't be abandoned or rejected and can be called upon when they are needed in the future.

After letting go of protective (fearful) subparts, the wound needs to be fully experienced and accepted.

3. Experiencing grief and/or anger. Part of fully accepting the wound involves experiencing grief and anger over past losses that have not been fully digested. If there is an overabundance of grief that is prolonged, anger may need to be expressed before there is an ability to move on in the process. Sometimes a great deal of anger needs to be released verbally or through some type of physical release (pounding fists or hitting a bat against a cushion) before the grief can be fully embraced.

4. Sorrow. This stage is at the center of the healing process. As one opens up to the wounds of the self and others, one is able to experience greater empathy. There is a common boundary where there is a connection that was not there previously. One is able to "walk in the other's shoes" (whether it is an inner relationship (subpersonalities) or with a real person in the external world). The experience of sharing a deep appreciation for the other's suffering leads one to feel sorrow for the other. As one experiences sorrow for the other, many other powerful emotions can occur including remorse for alienating yourself from other parts of yourself or another actual person. There is a deep experience of grief which reflects tears of caring. These are also tears of cleansing the inner wounds.

In the Jewish mystical text of the Zohar (Book of Splendor), there is a passage that describes the process of feeling sorrow and its connection to the highest spirituality:

> The answer is that "from the day of the destruction of the Temple, all gates to heaven have been closed, but the gates of tears have not been closed," and suffering and sadness are expressed in tears. Standing over the gates of tears are certain heavenly beings, and they break down the bars and locks of iron, and allow the tears to enter, so that the entreaties of the grieving supplicants go through and reach the holy King, and the place of the Divine Presence is grieved by the sorrow of him who prays, as it stands written: "In all their afflictions He is afflicted. . ." (Isa. 63:9)[1]

Through weeping, one can discover a great deal about oneself, others, and spirituality, which aids healing. A Jewish mystic, Rabbi Eiezer Zeui Safrin discusses the relationship between weeping and secrets. Safrin makes remarks to the first volume of the Zohar, where he confesses:

> By much weeping, like a well, and suffering, I became worthy to be transformed into a flowing stream, a fountain of wisdom; no secret was revealed to me, nor a wondrous apprehension, but afterward I became like dust and wept before the creator of the universe like a spring, lest I should be rejected from the light of his face, and for the sake of gaining apprehensions out of the source of wisdom, and I became as a flowing well weeping. (Passage from *Kabbalah, New Perspectives*, Moishe Idel, p. 86)

5. Compassion. Paul (1966) in his work on the use of empathy in the resolution of grief discusses how the process of empathy enables the individual to transcend oneself and see the other as who he/she is. He states, "empathy . . . presupposes the existence of the other as a separate individual, entitled to her own feelings, ideas, and emotional history. The empathizer makes no judgments about what the other should feel but solicits the expression of whatever feelings may exist, and for brief periods feels them as his own . . . The empathetic relationship is generous; the empathizer does not use the object (other person) as a means for gratifying his own sense of self-importance, but is principally concerned with encouraging the other to sustain and express his feelings and fantasies as being appropriate to himself" (p. 154).

Working with empathetic compassion is the beginning of opening one's heart. Individuals can experience the living, pulsating, timeless presence of their own individual existence and simultaneously will experience the unity that exists between themselves and others. This kind of experience is at the apex of a deep spiritual connection.

Choygan Trungpa (1973) discusses the Buddhist approach of compassion as the "open way." He states, "opening one's self to life, being what you are, presenting your positive and negative qualities to your spiritual friend and working your way through is the Buddhist path" (p. 91). He also states that "compassion is the basic warmth . . . first with yourself which can lead to having greater understanding, trust, and inspiration to dance with life and to communicate with the energies of the world . . . compassion automatically invites you to relate with people because you no longer regard them as a negative influence on your energy" (p. 97, 98).

6. *Love.* The sorrow for the other and the corresponding compassion that one feels leads one to feeling a deep care, love, and bond that many times was not there previously. My work with clients has demonstrated that the love is experienced in the chest (heart chakra) where one feels a greater sense of breathing and expansion that is very calming and cleansing. There is often an experience of energy in the body moving upwards and outwards and a sense of lightness prevails. As the energy moves upward through the throat chakra, there is a need for expression of this love outwardly (this can be facilitated through inner dialogue or outer verbal expression with the subpersonalities or an actual real person).

7. *Forgiveness.* There is very little written about forgiveness in the psychology literature yet it is so central to the healing process. My experience with working with forgiveness is that it is not an all or none event. This process can happen many times and we reach new levels of forgiveness as our understanding of life widens. As we continue to experience our own or other's pain and are able to have more compassion toward ourselves and others, forgiveness is a natural process that emerges as a way to a final release from suffering. It is the process whereby we let go of our expectations of ourselves or others to be any different from what we were or others were in the past. Part of letting go of expectations is not forgetting what happened but accepting the events that occurred with understanding that we or others were ignorant of what effects we were having on ourselves and others.

As we let go of the expectations that we had of ourselves and others, a tremendous release occurs, gnawing pains and tensions throughout the body soften. There is a tremendous inflooding of abundant positive energy. As I discussed previously under the stage of love, the inner chakras continue to open up and the therapist can help to facilitate this process by tracking what is going on in the body from moment to moment. Clients experience abundant energy in their body moving upward from the chest, throat, and upward through and around the head. There is an experience of lightness and expansion. Many of the higher qualities of the superconscious that were discussed previously in the last chapter can fully be realized as one transforms the inner family. It is useful to have clients affirm these experiences by using affirmations that come directly out of their experience such as stating, "I am joy, harmony, understanding, love, etc." These qualities are at the apex of our spiritual nature.

In closing, this notion of tracking clients' experience in their body as they release their inner wounds and open to compassion, love, and forgiveness has been ignored a great deal in traditional psychotherapy and yet these are the most profound experiences that can transform and add greater meaning to our lives.

PROCEDURES FOR HEALING INTRAGENERATIONAL WOUNDS

The process of healing intragenerational wounds also involves seven stages:

1. Aligning will with current symptoms,
2. Accessing the inner child,
3. Accessing the inner parents,
4. Accessing the inner parent's inner child,
5. Accessing the inner grandparent(s),
6. Return to the inner child and the inner parent of the client,
7. Healing the intragenerational images.

It is difficult to capture deep healing work in just explaining methods without the context of actual clinical material. Therefore, what follows in the next few chapters are excerpts from an intense therapeutic session that lasted about two and half hours which reflects the stages and procedures mentioned above. I am flexible with how long I see clients especially when powerful material that is ready to be healed has been emerging from previous sessions.

NOTE

1. Passage from *Zohar: The Book of Splendor. Basic Readings from the Kabbalah.* Edited by Gershom G. Scholem, p. 98.

Chapter 9

Accessing Inner Will

Working with the will was discussed in Chapter 6 as one tool to help with spiritual growth. Through meditation, one can begin to contemplate on the next steps in our growth process. As we begin to disidentify from our subparts and go deeper into our personal "I" or center, we get clearer on our individual direction.

Some meditation works on directing our attention to our breathing or emerging sensations in different places in our body. However, another type of meditation is concentrating deeply on thoughts that are surfacing in our consciousness. These thoughts can be directed toward future goals that are congruent with needs that are aligned with our essential core Self that wants us to achieve greater wholeness.

In this chapter we will begin to explore one clinical case in depth to demonstrate the different stages and procedures of healing the intragenerational family. This chapter will focus on the stage of accessing the client's inner will. I will briefly discuss the presenting problems of this case.

This session revolves around the grief over Sheila's boyfriend Bill, who committed suicide. Sheila is very depressed and has not been able to draw, which has been problematic because part of her career is as an artist.

ALIGNING WILL

In this first section, Sheila and I meditate together before we enter into a therapeutic dialogue; both of us have our eyes closed. This is to help reach and to align herself to work deeply. In this segment she has a preoccupation with her deceased boyfriend Bill.

ALIGNING WILL WITH CURRENT SYMPTOMS

Therapist: What I want you to do is just focus on your breath . . . be aware of the inhalation and exhalation of the breath . . . putting your bare attention on the inhaling and exhaling of your breath . . . and as you focus on your breath, what are you feeling right now?
Sheila: Well, I was also thinking about Bill.
Therapist: What's come up for you that has to do with Bill?
Sheila: How much I miss him and still feel about him even though he's gone. When I was meditating, I felt him all around me and I came in touch with the way I feel for him in my heart, even though he's not around me. You know when someone dies . . . you just assume the feelings are gonna leave, you don't expect . . .

Much of the letting go in healing work has to do with the heart center. In Chapter 6, I also discussed the "psycho-spiritual centers" found in the body that can be utilized as a focus of therapeutic healing, when a therapist tracks the client's sensations in the body as emotions are being experienced. It is amazing how the therapist and client can see and feel the connection between a psychological issue that is felt so deeply embedded in these various body centers. Since the client naturally mentioned her heart, it is often useful to introduce guided imagery work focusing on the body center or to have the client experience the imagery in the heart. The session proceeds with this kind of work.

Therapist: How do you feel about Bill in your heart? I'm wondering if you would try to do a little experiment to take you where you are right now with Bill in your heart.
Sheila: Uh-huh.
Therapist: Would you be willing to do that?
Sheila: Okay.
Therapist: See if you can focus on your heart right now and feel Bill in your heart and just see . . . as you sense Bill in your heart, express to me what's going on inside of you.
Sheila: Well, when I see him I want to laugh . . . because he's always so dramatic and in the back of that I'm still really sad because I can see him in my mind's eye but (begins to cry) . . . I'm never going to see him again physically . . . and I have a real loss

around that . . . it's not enough to feel him and see him in my mind's eye.

Therapist: What's going on inside right now, Sheila?

Sheila: I feel real sad and I need him to hold me. I haven't let go of him.

CLARIFYING THE WILL

In the next segment, I begin to activate her will to investigate her intention and purpose of this session. This is done by a series of questions as was mentioned previously. The first operation is clarification of emerging needs toward wholeness as well as direct inquires into intentionality and purpose which can help her motivation to work deeply. These questions help the client get closer to her personal "I" or "center" which is a space that is connected to the Higher Self which uniquely knows how to facilitate a self-completion process.

Therapist: Well, why don't you just come back here with me . . . and I know you've been struggling with this for some time now. What do you feel that you need to do to let go of Bill? And what do you feel like you need to do to heal?

Sheila: I don't want to let him go, so it's a double bind . . . you know, I want to be able to go on with my life and I don't want to let him go . . . so . . .

Therapist: Tell me more about how you want to go on with your life.

Sheila: Well, I want to be able to have another relationship . . . and I want to be able to go on with my work, in a focused way.

Therapist: So kind of having him inside of you distracts you from what your next step may be.

Sheila: Yes. Particularly from any other relationship.

Therapist: Tell me how life would be for you if perhaps you digest more of this loss, or how life would be if you had more direction toward where your next step would be.

Sheila: Tell you how life would be?

Therapist: Yes, tell me how life would be.

Sheila: Well, I feel like I'm having a creative block . . . that would be removed and I would be writing and I would be painting and I would be more creatively expressing myself than I have been.

As the client aligns her emerging needs and intentionality, she discovers a purpose and direction. Higher spiritual qualities can naturally emerge from the super-conscious such as the quality of hope.

Therapist: Okay, what are you experiencing right now?
Sheila: The possibilities . . . hope . . .
Therapist: I'd like for you to go inside (eyes closed) and experience some hope right now . . . see if you can deepen that experience of hope . . . there's all that energy curled up inside of you . . . wanting to be fully expressed . . . so what's happening right now?
Sheila: Well, I'm seeing all the times I don't work because I'm lethargic or depressed, you know, how good it does feel to be fully creative . . . and to use that . . . you know, I wish I could generate it at will . . . when it comes over me that I miss Bill.
Therapist: So there's a lot of hope and possibilities?
Sheila: Yes.
Therapist: Are you willing to maybe try to move to your next step now? Whatever that can be, are you willing to allow something new to happen, to move to the next step to which you have just created in front of you?
Sheila: Yes, definitely.

INTENTIONALITY WITH THE WILL

In this next section I am continuing to mobilize her will and deal with the possible positive outcome if she lets go of Bill. Creating this positive balance helps give courage to move into the deeper, painful healing work. This also aligns her direction with greater intention which gives her increased motivation.

Therapist: Now tell me what the benefits would be for you, if you could digest the stuff with Bill and get on with your creative process? Just tell me a little more about the benefits.

Sheila: Well, the benefits are endless because I have a lot of dangling projects that I can't get focused on to do.
Therapist: Can you just list those projects . . . just kind of free associate?
Sheila: Well, I have some paintings I'm working on, some drawings I'm working on . . . and I have a big video project I'm involved in and a community that I'm working with . . .
Therapist: So you're willing to move to the next step so some of these things can be manifested?
Sheila: Yes, I'd like to do that . . . I'd LOVE to do that (laughter).

MOBILIZING THE WILL

As the client gets more and more aligned with her direction in the session, the therapist helps to aid her in acknowledging a change toward the future. Emphasis is placed on grounding the intention and purpose by having the client state she is wanting or choosing to move in a certain direction. This helps to make her more responsible for her own work on herself.

Therapist: So you're choosing to do that right now?
Sheila: Yes, I choose to move to my next step.
Therapist: What I want to do next with you is for you to go inside of yourself . . . and see if you can now see what's blocking you from moving to your next step. See what comes.
Sheila: Oh, it's sadness and fear of going ahead with work that I'm doing right now . . . because the work that I'm doing is work that I was doing with Bill and things that we talked about . . . and I shared all my ideas with him . . . (crying).
Therapist: Just let that out.
Sheila: He's not here anymore, and I have to do it alone. I hate it!
Therapist: Is there something you hate in relationship to Bill?
Sheila: I hate the fact that he's gone!
Therapist: Can you express that to Bill? Right now can you see Bill in front of you? (She nods.) Say to him, "I hate that you're gone!"
(This is done in guided imagery.)

Sheila: "I HATE THAT YOU'RE GONE! You said you wouldn't leave!"

Therapist: Where do you feel the anger inside of you? I mean, where in your body?

Sheila: Kind of all over.

Therapist: Not more in one place?

Sheila: In my arms.

Therapist: Okay, focus on your arms right now and just let the anger go down your arms while you express it.

Sheila: "I resent your not being here . . . I resent your leaving me . . . I resent your telling me you weren't going to leave and then leaving . . . I RESENT YOUR DYING!"

Therapist: So what are you experiencing now?

Sheila: Calm, feeling calm.

Therapist: And where do you experience the calmness?

Sheila: In my chest.

There is already some emotional release from the letting go of anger. It is often very healing to continue to focus on that part of the body that has opened due to the letting go of negative emotions. Sheila still experiences this in her chest and I facilitate her deeply entering into her heart that has intuitive wisdom of where she needs to go with her own process. This is a good illustration of the integration of the use of meditation with psychotherapy.

The heart center is generally considered a focus of meditation. It is also a seat of wisdom. The therapist knows that he is deep in contact with that center when the client reports a state of expansiveness that emanates from that place in the body. This is clearly illustrated in the next clinical segment.

Therapist: See if you can focus on your chest, tune into the calmness and tell me what you are experiencing.

Sheila: I feel a kind of being expanded . . . and uh, peaceful . . . almost like . . .

Therapist: Okay, now just see if you can fully experience that relaxation now and from this space see if there's anything you need to work on with Bill right now, in this place right now, what needs to happen with you and Bill . . .

Sheila: Well, it seems to be real obvious, if I do the work that I've started to do, like the drawings . . . that it will help me resolve this . . .

Therapist: That's what's coming to you? If you can begin?

Sheila: It's like . . . I have to be willing to experience the pain . . . that I feel when I'm doing it . . .

Therapist: Okay, are you willing to take the next step? Are you able to see a picture of yourself right now, of yourself drawing a picture, in your studio? And then imagine yourself doing well and also imagine that Bill's gone.

Sheila: I miss him acutely. I'm lonely.

Chapter 10

Accessing the Intragenerational Family

This section will continue the stages and procedures of intragenerational family healing through clinical material. The sessions of Sheila will continue and will include strategies to access the inner child, the inner parents, inner parent's inner child, and the inner grandparents.

ACCESSING THE INNER CHILD

This process involves getting an image of the inner child. This process is done with eyes closed. Before one is instructed to image, one is asked to focus one's attention on the inhale and exhale of their breath (method to move into observing personal center or "I"). When one uses spontaneous images of painful parts of the self, many abstract, sometimes inanimate images such as a tightrope (which would represent a frightened child), a desert or empty house (which could symbolize a lonely, abandoned, sad child) emerge in the therapeutic work. As you work with the more abstract symbols and track where the pain is in the body, the child images will surface spontaneously.

Sometimes the inner child emerges spontaneously as part of an affective state that the client experiences. When the child image surfaces, the client is asked to describe what age the child is, what the child looks like, what he is wearing.

As the client gets focused on the image as if this image is external to himself (disidentification), he is then to ask to identify with that child, to imagine becoming this part. It is useful to have the client take two or three deep breaths when making any shift from disidentification to identification processes. He is then instructed that you (the therapist) will talk with this part. It is important to talk to this part as if you were really talking with a young child (in a gentle, soothing, yet firm, supportive voice). You ask the inner child how he got to be the way he is, what he wants and needs, etc. As you facilitate the inner child to talk, you ask what he is experiencing now and whether he is experiencing any strong sensation or affects emerging in the body. As emotions start to emerge, you tell the client once again to take some deep breaths and focus attention on the part of the body that is in pain and to continue to express what and how that pain is experienced.

The next section focuses on Sheila's lonely subpersonality that grips her and causes her to become very depressed. Work with this subpart is facilitated.

Therapist: Can you be in touch with that lonely part of yourself right now, the Lonely One.
Sheila: Uh-huh.
Therapist: Can you see that part of you?
Sheila: Yes.
Therapist: What's that part look like?
Sheila: A little girl.
Therapist: Can you describe the little girl to me?
Sheila: She's all dressed up in a little pink dress . . . black patent leather shoes and she's by herself . . .
Therapist: She's by herself? How old is she?
Sheila: About two and a half or three.
Therapist: Two and a half or three. And she's very lonely?
Sheila: Uh-huh.

The following is instructing her to fully identify with the image in order to access the pain. In addition, I dialogue directly with her inner child.

Therapist: Okay, now what I want you to do is see if you can allow yourself to imagine that you are the two-and-a-half- or three-year-old little girl in the pink dress and I want you to talk to me and tell me about your loneliness.
Sheila: "My father doesn't like me."

Therapist: He doesn't like you. (Therapist talks directly to the sub-part.) "Tell me, little girl, Lonely One, what it's like for your father not to like you."

Sheila: "He doesn't give me any attention, he ignores me unless he's being mean to me, so I . . . I want him to like me."

Therapist: "What's it like, Lonely One, to be ignored by your daddy?"

Sheila: "It's scary."

ACCESSING THE INNER PARENT(S)

As the inner child explores his inner experience, there will usually be conflict with one or both parents. This will spontaneously occur, and as issues with the parents naturally emerge, you continue to facilitate a dialogue with the internal image of the parent.

The process of accessing the internal parental image is by asking if the client can get an image of the parent. One asks what the parent looks like, what he/she is wearing, what mood is the parent experiencing, etc. The client then is instructed to take a few deep breaths and focus on the image of the parent external to himself and speak to this parent from the inner identification with the inner child. During this dialectical process powerful affects can emerge including grief/anger that was previously described. It is important to get the child to talk directly to the internal parent, especially of his unmet needs.

The next segment begins to direct the client into embracing other familial (father) images in order to begin the practice of subpersonality (inner family) coordination which is opening up a dialogue between intragenerational fragments.

Therapist: Okay, now I want you to get a picture of Daddy in front of you. Do you have a picture of Daddy?

Sheila: Uh-huh.

Therapist: Now say, "Daddy, I'm scared."

Sheila: I'm afraid to do that.

Therapist: Take some deep breaths. Take some deeper breaths. Remember what goals you had? (Breathes, encouraged to let go of fear)

Sheila: (Crying) It's hard to say that.

Therapist: Okay, tell your daddy it's hard to talk to him right now.

Sheila: I'm afraid that he'll get angry.

Therapist: Okay . . . tell him that you're afraid to say it because you think he might get angry with you.

Sheila: "I'm afraid that if I say these things then, Daddy, you'll get angry with me . . ."

Therapist: What are you experiencing now as you say that to Daddy?

Sheila: I'm getting worried.

Therapist: What are you worried that might happen to you now? As you look at him now?

Sheila: I am going to hide.

Therapist: Where would you hide?

Sheila: In my bed.

Therapist: In your bed. With the covers over?

Sheila: Yes.

Therapist: Okay. Can you imagine that this is your bed?

Sheila: That's my bed?

Therapist: Would you be willing to lay down? (Sheila actually lays down in that position to amplify the process.) Sheila, what I'd like you to do is imagine again the two-and-a half- or three-year-old "Lonely One" there now hiding from Daddy. Now tell me what you're feeling as you're hiding.

Sheila: I'm feeling afraid that he's going to find me.

Therapist: "I'm afraid that my dad is going to find me." Now just verbalize that. "I'm afraid, Daddy, that you're going to find me."

Sheila: "I'm afraid, Daddy, that you're going to find me."

Therapist: Now, where do you experience the fear right now?

Sheila: In my stomach.

As the therapist once again focuses on the bodily experiences of the client, the "psycho-spiritual" centers can be released. The client gets in touch with fear of dialoguing with her inner father and feels this in her stomach area (navel center) which is the seat of power versus helplessness in the Eastern chakra system. By the therapist helping the client continue to attend to this part of the body, she can experience greater, quicker, deeper, and more profound healing work.

Therapist: So just focus on your stomach right now, take some deep breaths right there . . . okay, now, say "I'm scared," and talk from your stomach, "I'm scared, Daddy." . . . all right?

Sheila: I–I'm scared. I don't want to talk with him.

Therapist: You don't want to talk with him. Then say, "I don't want to talk with you."

Sheila: He wouldn't let me talk.

Therapist: How are you feeling towards Dad?

Sheila: I feel fine as long as I'm here and the door's shut! I'm afraid if I talk to him, he'll come in!

Therapist: Let's make pretend right now, totally where you're at, that Daddy won't come in.

Sheila: Daddy won't come in?

Therapist: Daddy won't come in. And see if you can express what's there in your stomach.

Sheila: I see a big ball.

The next section works with the big ball which is a protective part of Sheila that is resisting moving into focus. As this part is recognized and accepted, it moves aside for Sheila to continue her work. In healing work, resistances are viewed as other subparts that need to be embraced, accepted, and worked with cooperatively.

Therapist: Now, just experience that big ball for right now in your stomach.

Sheila: It's really tight.

Therapist: Just experience that tightness in your stomach right now.

Sheila: It's like I have to hold onto it.

As the image of the big ball is increasingly accepted, a new image appears of a tunnel which appears to act as a protector of Sheila's frightened inner child. As the tunnel emerges as a symbol of protection, the therapist asks that the image of the tunnel and the lonely child dialogue with each other. The third phase of subpart work after recognition and acceptance is coordinating the needs of the two parts. When a dominant protective part is recognized and accepted it can listen to other vulnerable parts and give space for the less developed fearful parts to grow.

Therapist: Now speak from that ball, what the experience is like to be inside that ball. "I . . ."

Sheila: I am condensed . . . it feels real solid in there.

Therapist: Okay, now stay with that right there. Okay, stay with the condensedness, and whatever is going on inside you with that condensedness.

Sheila: Yes, I feel condensed and dark . . . hard . . . flat . . . real heavy and kind of stable, like without that, somehow I would disappear.

Therapist: Now I want you to image that hardness in your stomach right now . . . see if you can imagine what that part is. . . did an image come?

Sheila: Kind of an interesting image of a tunnel; a place to hide.

Therapist: A tunnel? Now, why don't you talk from this tunnel, become this tunnel and talk to the Lonely One and tell the Lonely One all you have done to keep the Lonely One together.

Sheila: You mean like, I've given you someplace to hide.

Therapist: Yes. Uh-huh.

Sheila: "I've given you someplace to hide. I've given *you* something to hold onto."

Therapist: Can you tell her what else you've given her?

Sheila: "I've given you a place to put your desperate fear, a place to go when you're scared . . . I've given you a place to put all of that . . . all of that pain that you feel and I've given you a place to put all those tears."

Therapist: And what else do you feel for the little girl?

Sheila: Sorry for her.

Therapist: Could you tell her that?

Sheila: "I feel really sorry for you; I think you are very sweet. I'm sorry you're so scared."

The following is a continued dialogue between subparts; the tunnel-protector and the frightened child. The frightened, lonely child accepts the tunnel-protector and expresses love as the protective part tries to let go.

Therapist: Now, have the little girl talk to the tunnel and this protector and see how she responds to this "tunnel-protector." See what she needs to express.

Sheila: "Well, I'm glad that you did that."

Therapist: And, "Lonely One, what do you need from the tunnel-protector?"

Sheila: "Well, I guess that I've learned a lot and I need for you to let me go."

Therapist: Okay, now talk to this part, this tunnel, and talk about your need for it to give you more room.

Sheila: "I need for you to open WAY up and not be so tough, in fact . . ."

Therapist: Say, "I need for you to open WAY UP."

Sheila: "I need you to open WAY up. I love you, but you need to let me do more."

Therapist: See if you can give the tunnel a voice and talk back to the little girl, just to see what she wants from you.

Sheila: "Well, I've been here for a long time and it's kind of hard to leave. I'm not sure you can take care of yourself, and you might not have a place to go if I leave. I'm afraid that you may be lonely."

Therapist: What does the little girl say?

Sheila: "I don't need you anymore. I'm not afraid of Daddy anymore. "

It is easier for coordination of parts to occur when there is a feeling of mutual respect and both parts feel they are not going to be destroyed; on the contrary, they can both continue to see their usefulness to one another.

Therapist: Is there anything you need from this part? Anything you need to take along your journey? Has this part played a special role in your life?

Sheila: The only thing I can think about is that I'd like to take along the feeling of love that . . . and I could take along the feeling of knowing that you served a useful purpose and that I could take along the feeling of not having felt bad.

Therapist: Sheila, have your lonely child ask your tunnel-protector if it would give you space now to grow.

Sheila: "Please give me an opportunity to take care of myself and heal." Tunnel-protector says, "Yes, I will give you space if you promise you'll come back to me if you need me." Lonely child says, "Okay, I love you"(starts crying). "Thanks for being there for me."

Therapist: Sheila, I'd like you to take a deep breath . . . come over here and . . . I want to help you up . . . and come over here–you're doing some good work.

Sheila sits up and continues imagining her inner father and the inner family work continues. The next segment works on her letting go of fear and experiencing her underlying feelings of anger and rage. This section is a very powerful affective part that aims at strong cathartic discharge that is part of the healing process.

Therapist: What do you want to say to your father?
Sheila: "I don't have to be scared of you anymore . . ."
Therapist: Okay, take some deep breaths.
Sheila: I see him when he's about 33, and he's 76 right now.
Therapist: It was when you were scared of him, when he was 33?
Sheila: Probably.
Therapist: Okay, imagine that he's 33.
Sheila: It's hard to look.
Therapist: Okay, there's still a part of that fear here, so would you take some of that protection and courage and express to him some of what you've never expressed?
Sheila: "I hate your guts."
Therapist: Okay, say it again.
Sheila: "I hate your guts."
Therapist: Tell him what you hate about him.
Sheila: "I hate it that you're so big and you're so mean . . . you hit my mother . . . and I hate that you blame it on everybody else . . ."
Therapist: Did he ever blame it on you?
Sheila: Yes.
Therapist: Can you tell him you're not to blame?
Sheila: "I'm not to blame for your hitting my mother."
Therapist: Say it again!
Sheila: "I'm not to blame for your hitting my mother."
Therapist: Louder.
Sheila: "I'M NOT TO BLAME FOR YOU HITTING MY MOTH-ER!"
Therapist: Say it again.
Sheila: "I hate you. I'm not to blame for your hitting my mother."
Therapist: What's going on right now?

Sheila: Well, he drank. That's why he hit my mother. He accused us and told us it was our fault that he hit her.
Therapist: How are you feeling now as you talk to Dad?
Sheila: Vengeful (laughter). I'd like to kick him, bite him. "I'd like to stomp on your guts. I'd like to burn you with cigarettes."
Therapist: All the things you wanted to say when you were a kid.
Sheila: "I'd like to scream and yell until you go crazy. I would like to take you and hold you down in your bed."
Therapist: "I'd like to hold you down on YOUR bed."
Sheila: "I'd like to hold you down on YOUR bed and make it so you can't get up. I'd like to rub a diaper in your face, so you can see how it feels. I'd like to rub a diaper in your face. I'd like to throw food at you; I'd like to pour milk down your mouth so fast you can't drink it. I would just like to do all the things to you that you've done to me!"

The next process of Stage 3–accessing the inner parent–involves reversing images of the internal parent and child (so the child becomes the externalized image and the parental images become the objects of identification). Before you reverse the images, one instructs the client to take a few deep breaths. The client is asked to put the image of the child outside of himself and to identify fully with the inner parent and the parent is urged to dialogue back to the inner child. It is important to get the parent's first name and after the parental image responds to the inner child, the therapist engages in a dialogue with the internal parent and calls him by his first name and asks a series of questions such as if he has been attached to a subpart of himself (i.e., critic, aloof, distant, etc., subpersonality). The therapist continues to dialogue with the subpart of the parent and asks him how he has become the way he has been with his child/spouse, etc. This inevitably leads to this part's pain related to its family of origin experience. Much emotion can be expressed as this process is facilitated.

To further demonstrate, Sheila's inner father is imaged, and the therapist dialogues with that image to further facilitate internal family integration.

Therapist: Okay, take a couple deep breaths and allow for images. Identify with your father and put little Sheila outside of you (all

done with eyes closed). Now, I'm going to talk with your inner father. "Did you hear what your daughter said. How do you feel?"
Sheila: (Speaking from voice of Phil–inner father) "I am deeply saddened by all the pain I caused Sheila. I just have felt burdened and hurt all my life."
Therapist: "Why has your life been so full of pain?"
Sheila: (As inner father) "I had no father and my mother was too busy chasing guys. She was so sad so much of the time. I tried to comfort her. I didn't know how. I was so little and lonely. I was lonely and unloved" (starts to cry).

ACCESSING THE INNER PARENT'S INNER CHILD

The inner parent usually can spontaneously express childhood hurts. The inner parent is instructed to get an image of the inner child within themselves. The same process as has been explained previously when the client imagined his own inner child is done here.

The next section focuses on Sheila's doing intragenerational work beginning with guided imagery with her internal father's inner child and his mother (her internal grandmother).

Sheila: (Inner child of father speaks to his mother) "My life's been full of a lot of pain because of all the men you had . . . you've not been a good mother . . . you went to church every Sunday and acted like you're real religious but you have all these different men and you don't care how they treat you . . . you let them beat up on you."

I talk directly with Sheila's inner father's (Phil) child's image. The beginning of healing takes place as Sheila lets go of her father's grief and anger, which is also her own grief and pain.

Therapist: How are you feeling, Phil, when you're talking to your mom?
Sheila: My father feels like he wants to beat her up.
Therapist: "I'm angry with you, Mom."
Sheila: "I'm angry with you, Mom, for not taking care of me and for having all those men . . . and giving all your money to the church

. . . I'm mad at you for not giving me all the attention I needed and I'm angry at you for not loving me and I'm angry at you for beating me."

Therapist: What did you need from . . . Mom, Phil?

Sheila: "I needed her to love me."

Therapist: Okay, say that, "Mom, I really needed you to love me."

Sheila: "I really needed you to love me. I needed you to think about me . . . not just yourself."

Therapist: What's going on inside?

Sheila: It's a real strange feeling . . . it's hard to describe . . . just seeing my father interact with his mother and knowing it's true . . . at another level.

Therapist: See if you can allow yourself to focus more on Phil right now, more on your dad. Can you see a picture of him now?

Sheila: Yeah, it's like he wants to please her. He tries everything to please her and nothing matters.

Therapist: Okay, say, "Mom, I try to please you but nothing matters."

Sheila: "Mom, I try to please you but nothing matters. I don't get your attention; you don't care . . . it seems like the only attention I can get is when you're hitting me."

Therapist: Can you tell Mom how it felt to get hit, Phil?

Sheila: Well, it hurt . . . but there's almost a sense of satisfaction because at least she's paying some attention to me.

Therapist: Do you feel some hurt right now?

Sheila: Uh-huh.

Therapist: Where do you feel it?

Sheila: In my chest.

Therapist: You feel Daddy's hurt, right? Of not being loved.

Sheila: Uh-huh.

Therapist: See if you can talk to his mommy, "Mommy, I'm feeling hurt."

Sheila: "I'm really hurt, Mommy, and I'm really angry with you. I feel sorry for you, but I need some care."

Therapist: Say it again. "I'm really sorry for you, but I need some care."

Sorrow, as was discussed previously, for the other is the beginning of opening up one's compassionate heart, and healing can progress. In this next segment, the client experiences her inner father's heart open toward his mother (her internal grandmother). Part of opening the heart center can involve letting go of fear, anger, and grief as is illustrated here.

Sheila: "I need some attention and I need some care. I need to be held."
Therapist: Tell Mom what it feels like not to be held and cared for.
Sheila: "It feels real scary. It feels like I'm supposed to be able to do everything by myself without any help . . . like I've been abandoned . . . it feels like you don't love me and it feels real scary."
Therapist: Where do you experience that feeling?
Sheila: In my heart.
Therapist: Okay, now focus on your heart; take some deep breaths and say, "I'm scared, Mom."
Sheila: "I'm scared."
Therapist: Just experience that.
Sheila: "I'm scared. I'm scared of all those men. I'm scared of all those different men . . . I'm scared of what they do to you . . . I'm scared because they take you away . . . and I'm alone."
Therapist: You're left alone.
Sheila: (Nods.)
Therapist: So you have a lonely part of you, too, Phil.
Sheila: Real alone.

ACCESSING THE INNER GRANDPARENT

The inner parent's inner child is asked to get a picture of his internal parent(s) (the client's grandparent) and externalize this picture outwardly. As the client identifies with his own parent's inner child, once again he is asked to engage in a dialogue now with his inner grandparent. Affects are tracked as well as where any pain is located in the body. As was described previously, images are reversed so the inner parent's child and the parent's parent can have a chance to dialogue. It is also important to get the client's grandparent's first name so the therapist can dialogue directly with the grandparental image. Some clients never knew their grandparent, however, one still facilitates this process with imaging what they imagined the grandparent looked like, etc. Many people carry around these sub-parts unconsciously through photographs that they saw as children of their grandparents or by stories and attitudes from their parents about their own parents. As the inner parent's inner child hears the story of their inner grandparent, the stages of healing start to be perpetuated whereby the inner parent's inner child starts to feel sorrow for his inner parent (client's grandparent). The heart chakra often begins to open and the experience of love and forgiveness occurs. This process is experienced by many clients as very awesome; they are finishing their parent's unfinished business with their parents.

Stage 5 process can be repeated with some success with some clients with imaging the inner child of great-grandparents dialoguing with the inner child of the great-great-grandparents.

In the next segment Sheila's inner father's (Phil) inner mother dialogues with the therapist.

Sheila: (Inner grandmother) (Starts to cry.) "I am so sorry. I didn't know what I was doing. I had nobody."
Therapist: (Therapist talks directly to inner grandmother of Sheila) What was it like to have nobody?
Sheila: "My husband beat me. I had to work and no one looked after me. I always had to take care of others since I was young. I guess I depended on Phil too much. (Starts to cry deeply.) I did the best I could."

The next stage of experiencing sorrow for the other continues the healing process. Intragenerational work continues as the therapist returns to the image of the inner child of father.

Therapist: (To inner child of father) Do you need to say anything to your mom?
Sheila: (As father) I feel sorry for her.
Therapist: Tell her that. "I feel sorry for you."
Sheila: "I feel sorry for you." She doesn't have anyone.
Therapist: She's pretty lonely too?
Sheila: Yes . . . in spite of all those men she doesn't have anybody who cares about her.
Therapist: Tell her how that makes you feel.

Sheila: Like she has to raise the family by herself.

Therapist: Can you feel that sorrow inside? Where do you experience it?

Sheila: In my chest. (opening up of heart chakra)

Therapist: Yes, see if you can express that sorrow towards your mom (client's inner grandmother).

Sheila: In my chest.

Therapist: See if you can express that sorrow towards your mom.

Sheila: (She cries a great deal.)

Therapist: Do you have any other feelings?

Sheila: Empathy. I hurt for my mom.

Therapist: Okay, stay with that. Say, "Mom, I hurt for you."

Sheila: "Mom, I hurt when I think about your situation . . . I feel really sorry for you."

Therapist: What's happening now?

Sheila: I just feel real sad.

Therapist: Say, "Mom, I feel really sad about your life."

Sheila: "Mom, I feel really sad about your life. I wish I could do something."

Therapist: Good. Do you feel that pain that's inside of your dad?

Sheila: Yes.

Therapist: How do you feel toward your mom now, Phil?

Sheila: "I wish I could help her."

Therapist: Uh-huh. Just tell her now. Say, "I wish I could help you."

Sheila: "I wish I could help you, but . . . I'm too little and helpless."

Therapist: Is there anything you want to say to her? As her son?

Sheila: "I love you."

Therapist: "I love you, Mom."

Sheila: "I love you, Mom." It's hard.

Therapist: Uh-huh. Can you forgive Mom for anything that she's done? She's made life pretty rough. She had a pretty rotten life herself. Could you tell her that?

Sheila: "I forgive you, Mom; it's okay" (extreme crying). "I feel so sorry for you."

Chapter 11

Transforming the Intragenerational Family

In this chapter, the final stages of inner transformation are explored. As one works through the stages of healing and embracing one's pain through letting go of fear, sorrow, grief, and rage, there are more positive qualities that emerge including compassion, love, and forgiveness. As these higher qualities are realized, one can utilize this positive affective experience to further heal all the original wounded images of the internal family. The last two stages of healing are demonstrated as we come to the end of Sheila's healing of her intragenerational family. The closing healing stages begin with going back to the original images of the client's inner child and inner parent.

RETURN TO THE INNER CHILD
AND THE INNER PARENT OF THE CLIENT

During this phase, there is a shift to the early images of the client's own inner child and parental images. Sometimes the images change or else they remain the same. The inner child is instructed to look at the parent's image and ask what the child is experiencing toward his parent. The same last three stages of the healing process occur. The inner child has tremendous understanding of the common themes and fetters that link the generations together. As this has been experienced, compassion, including sorrow and care for the parent, is realized. One then sets the stage for the expression of love and forgiveness to also be experienced. There may also be need for imaging the inner child or the image of the adult's current self, to work on self-forgiveness.

In the next section Sheila shuttles back to the image of her current father and she dialogues with him. Further healing work is realized as she experiences greater compassion, love, and forgiveness for him.

Therapist: What are you experiencing when you image Dad now?
Sheila: "I feel sorry for you, Daddy." (Crying) "I feel really sorry for you."
Therapist: Just say it again, tell what you feel sorry about.
Sheila: "I feel sorry that you grew old so fast, that your mother beat you, and all those men in your life that used to beat you."
Therapist: You feel sorry for his lost childhood.
Sheila: "I feel sorry for your lost childhood. I feel sorry for . . . your life. I feel sorry for the fact that you are old and unhappy."
Therapist: Is there anything you want to express to him? Right now? Okay, just experience that and say it.
Sheila: "I love you."
Therapist: What's happening now?
Sheila: Mm . . . I feel kind of wet in here . . . there are a lot of tears in here.
Therapist: Inside your heart? (She nods.) Okay, just feel the wet in there . . . now allow all the wetness to come out and tell Dad all the feeling that's there.
Sheila: "I know you did the best you could, but it wasn't very good. But I know you did the best you could."
Therapist: Can you tell him the loss you felt from the kind of father he was? Tell him the things you wish he would have done with you.
Sheila: "I wish you would have liked me when I was little, and I wish that you had been affectionate, and I wish that you had been proud of me. I wish that you had been loving and tender and that you'd cared about me, and I wish that you had been able to express your feelings of love as well as hate. And I wish that you had been able to hold me."

In the next segment, Sheila is experiencing the loss and grieving of her father not being able to nurture her the way she wanted him to. Sheila also gains insight between her grief over her father and her deceased boyfriend.

Therapist: Experience that loss right now. (Part of healing is letting go of losses.) Go ahead, Sheila. (Crying) It's a loss that you had as a child. Let it out, it's okay. You're mourning a childhood that you didn't have. What's happening now, Sheila?

Sheila: I was thinking about Bill and his being mixed up together with my father. (Many times spontaneous insights occur in inner family work.)

Therapist: How do you feel you are mixing them up?

Sheila: Well, Bill used to hold me.

Therapist: Oh, Bill used to hold you.

Sheila: And talk to me and do all those things that my daddy didn't do.

Therapist: So he was like a daddy to you.

Sheila: Probably. He really loved me. Yes, all aspects of the lost little girl, the scared little girl. I miss him for that.

Therapist: Before we move away from Dad, is there anything you want to say to Dad? (It's good to keep the process tracked.)

Sheila: Yeah, well, I guess, now that . . . he was a teacher for me . . . I am who I am because of the childhood I had with my father. There's a lot of pain there and I didn't like it, but I do like who I am now.

The next segment illustrates the last phase of healing which is exoneration and forgiving. After Sheila is able to let go of fear, anger, and grief, she is able to feel compassion and love. In this session she releases her father by affirming statements of forgiveness towards him.

Therapist: Tell him. "I do like who I am."

Sheila: "I do like who I am now and I realize you did the best you could do. I always thought you came into my life to teach me a lot of hard lessons, and I learned a lot of hard lessons from you . . ." I acknowledge him for being my father.

Therapist: Do you forgive him?

Sheila: Yes, I forgive him.

Therapist: Say, "Dad, I forgive you."

Sheila: "Dad, I forgive you."

Therapist: Is there anything else you need to say to him?

Sheila: "I just hope that you realize before you die that none of us

really hated you; we just feel sorry for you. You really did the best job you could do."
Therapist: He probably did, too. He had a lot of pain. He probably did the best he could do.

It is useful to go back to the original images to see if transformation took place in the inner child as a result of inner family work. After internal family healing work, there often is a flood of positive energy experience in the body. It's useful to continue to track this energy and facilitate the spontaneous waves of higher qualities of the supraconscious. Often this opening up of the body is accompanied by archetypal images. In Sheila's case, she receives images of white light beings (archetypal angel images) that further aid in her inner healing.

Therapist: Okay, are you ready to take the next step? See if you can go inside and picture this little girl who was hurt. Can you see her now? What does she look like?
Sheila: She has a pink dress on and patent leather shoes; she's playing on a swing.
Therapist: Swinging? Like back and forth?
Sheila: Yes.
Therapist: Okay, see if you can get in contact with that playfulness right now . . . even move your body–swing if you like.
Sheila: Okay, I'm in the swing.
Therapist: Swinging?
Sheila: Yes, I feel my swinging back and forth.
Therapist: Now, what's that quality right now?
Sheila: It's great.
Therapist: What are you experiencing right now?
Sheila: Freedom.
Therapist: Freedom. How does it feel to embrace that freedom right now?
Sheila: It feels good.
Therapist: Okay, now take some deep breaths and allow that quality of freedom to be there inside of you.
Sheila: Mm . . . I like it. It feels good.
Therapist: Open yourself up more to freedom. Take some deep breaths and open up . . . take another deep breath . . . feel the quality

of freedom and see if you can deepen that quality. What are you experiencing now?

Sheila: I feel very light.

Therapist: Stay with that lightness and move more into that lightness and see what comes . . . what comes to you . . . what's happening?

In this next section, the therapist continues to track the client's meditation experiences. He continues to facilitate her experiences through archetypal imagery from the supraconscious which are the white light angelic-like beings. These images are indicators that the higher unconscious continues to be tapped. The therapist utilizes these archetypal symbols for healing the early wounded childhood images.

Sheila: I have an image of . . . these white light beings . . .

Therapist: Just allow that image of white light beings to be there . . . what's happening now to that image?

Sheila: They are loving that little girl. They are just skipping over to her and loving her.

Therapist: All right. Now just put that little girl under those white light beings . . . and let that love be there for that little girl who tried so hard to be, who struggled. In fact let that light heal that little girl. Take some deep breaths. What are you experiencing now?

Sheila: They're hugging the little girl.

Therapist: Okay, just experience the hug. What are you experiencing in your body now?

Sheila: A feeling of being real light.

Therapist: Where do you experience that lightness?

Sheila: Kind of all over.

Therapist: Okay, just let yourself experience it all over your body as you focus on the little girl and the white light figures.

Sheila: Uh-huh.

Therapist: Move more into that quality. What are you experiencing now?

Sheila: Joy.

Therapist: Okay, now stay with joy. Experience joy . . . what's happening now?

Sheila: (Laughter) She's being absorbed into them.

Therapist: Feel, feel the little girl just in touch with the light . . . just free and joyous.
Sheila: Yeah, it's really powerful.
Therapist: Enjoy the freedom, the power, and talk from that quality. Say, "I am joy" and see if you can freely express what that quality is like in your body right now.

Sheila has a direct experience of spirituality through her supraconscious, higher qualities and she is encouraged to identify and affirm them from moment to moment.

Sheila: "I am joy, light; I am infinite possibilities . . . I am love, I am laughter, I am space . . ."
Therapist: Take some deep breaths.
Sheila: "I am absolute forgiveness and trust . . . I'm a feeling of being connected to another human being."
Therapist: What are you experiencing now?
Sheila: I'm kind of experiencing a settling down. (This is not an unusual experience after consciousness has been expanded.)
Therapist: Okay, just let that settling down happen. Take some breaths and allow yourself to settle. What's that like?
Sheila: I'm feeling really present.
Therapist: Feeling really present.
Sheila: Yes, kind of like supported and really present.

HEALING THE INTRAGENERATIONAL IMAGES

After the different stages between the generations has taken place and the above six stages have been experienced, the total process can be integrated with the following exercise:

Close your eyes, focus your attention on your breathing in and out of your nostrils. If your attention wanders, blow a little harder through your nose and bring your concentration back to one point beneath your nose where the air gently moves in and out. Take a deep breath through your nose quickly, hold it, and let it out slowly through your mouth (do this three times). Come back to your breathing in and out of your nostrils.

Allow an image of all of your family members to come to you, including yourself, siblings, parents, and grandparents (can include others, i.e., great-grandparents if appropriate). Put the image of everyone inside the middle of your chest (heart) and breathe in and out from that point. Hold your family in your heart.

Imagine a white, shining, glowing light above your head. Bring the light down through the top of your heart, through your forehead, face, neck and let it fill up the center of your heart. Hold the light and your family in your heart as you breathe in and out. See what happens to the inner images. If they need to talk to one another or do something with each other, allow this to happen.

(After a few minutes.) Allow the light to move up and out and blend into the atmosphere. Let the inner family image go knowing that you can return to this image at any time. Come back to your breathing gently through your nose. When you're ready, open your eyes.

This exercise can be used with any kind of inner family work as previously has been addressed, e.g., the inner nuclear family, inner parental marriage, inner siblings, etc. It is useful to use after there has been a coordinating and integration of the different images, especially after there has been an emotional release. It is also useful to track the client's sensations emerging in the body. As has been previously stated in the stages of healing after emotional release work from the inner family images occur, an influx of superconscious energies can be experienced and the highest of spiritual qualities can be realized.

In the next segment, Sheila is given the above directions for further intragenerational healing. She is facilitated through meditation and guided imagery to imagine her grandmother, father, and herself in the center of her chest facilitated with the sensation of light permeating the image. Further spiritual qualities are experienced as she embraces inner family unity.

Therapist: What are you experiencing as you hold your family in your chest?

Sheila: (Starts to cry) My grandmother, father, and I are all holding hands.
Therapist: Stay with the image and what is going on in your body.
Sheila: We are all dancing in a circle. (She spontaneously sings a childhood melody.)
Therapist: What are you experiencing?
Sheila: Joy. (Her body and face appear extremely open.) Everything feels together–whole–I never ever felt this inside. I feel unity and pulsating love and a feeling of oneness. I'm feeling alive and fully present and I am feeling solidly supported inside.

It is good to go back to the original problem, which was that of her deceased boyfriend. This can often help ground the work in what needs to be done practically in everyday life.

Therapist: Okay, feel that supported presence inside your body right now. And what I'd like you to do right now is maybe you can say to Bill, "I can have my own support. I am my own support." Something like that.
Sheila: "I can have my own support. I do have my own support."
Therapist: "I do have my own support."
Sheila: "I feel complete."
Therapist: Can you tell Bill what you can take from him and your relationship and what you can do to continue on your path? With your own support?
Sheila: "I can take . . . I can take the love" (crying).
Therapist: You can take his love?
Sheila: Yes, I can take the love.
Therapist: Anything else you can take?
Sheila: Yes, I can take everything that we talked about, and all the experiences that we had.
Therapist: Tell him that–"I can take all the experiences that we had."
Sheila: Right. "I can take all the experiences that we had together and move on in my life."

In the next segment, Sheila spontaneously transforms her symptoms of a drawing block and asks to draw on a blackboard that is in the room. She is able to regain the spirit of her inner child and draws the image of her own internal little girl swinging from a tree on top of a tunnel with angels figures flying over her.

Therapist: What are you experiencing now?

Sheila: I'm getting an image of that little girl and it's like I have to be wanting to trust that she's all right, that she's taking care of herself.

Therapist: Okay, just talk with the little girl and ask her what she wants from you.

Sheila: Well, she says it's her thing and I need to be able to trust that she can take care of herself and that she's okay. I need to quit worrying about her so much.

Therapist: Is there anything else that the little girl wants you to know?

Sheila: Yes, that when I do my art is when she's the happiest.

Therapist: Okay, good, now just fill yourself with that happiness. It's the way the little girl expresses herself, the way she creates. What's happening now?

Sheila: I feel like I want to go draw. I gotta leave (laughter); I've got work to do. (She breaks through the symptom of a creative block she has been experiencing.)

Therapist: Would you be willing to draw a picture on the board?

Sheila: Sure.

Therapist: I thought maybe you could just draw what this was like for you.

Sheila: Yeah.

Therapist: Here's the chalk.

Sheila: (She draws) This is like that tunnel and right here is the figure as I imaged it and a kind of glow. And the little girl got in here on the swing . . . it's really great.

Therapist: Okay, how do you feel now?

Sheila: I feel real light and I'm breathing a lot better and as if a huge weight has lifted off my shoulders.

Therapist: You look a little lighter.

Sheila: Yeah? I feel a lot lighter. A lot.

Therapist: Sheila, I'd like to ask you one last thing, okay?

The next brief section is continuing grounding her on how she can utilize these experiences in her daily life. This is done through a regular conversation–no imagery or eyes closed.

Sheila: Okay.

Therapist: Tell me what you've learned from this experience and really what you could do in your life right now to ground it, to even ground this experience more.

Sheila: I think one thing is to be willing to realize that I'm not going to be overwhelmed with the pain, that I can have the feeling but I don't have to become the feelings and I don't have to become totally lost and absorbed in it, which is sometimes how I feel–like I'm just in a wave of it and it's too much for me to experience. That's the feeling that I've had. If I experience the loss it will be just too much and I don't feel that way anymore. It's really tied up with the childhood energy; it's really tied up with being that little girl. Not being able to experience all the pain there and the pain now is different from the pain there and now there seems to be a separation.

Therapist: What can you do practically today to take from this experience and help you move into your next step?

Sheila: Well, I need to work on the drawings I've been working on.

Therapist: What will you need to remember that will really help you keep moving?

Sheila: Mm, to hold the picture of the little girl swinging and to know that I don't have to be overwhelmed.

Therapist: So maybe at times when you're feeling bogged down or overwhelmed you can image the energy of the little girl on the swing and you can choose to go your own way.

Sheila: Yes.

Therapist: Is there anything else you want to share? About what this has been like for you?

Sheila: Mm, well, it's so amazing and it feels like it's been very healing.

Chapter 12

Bridging Inner and Outer Family Healing

Our outer patterns in our intimate transactions with others precisely reflect our inner family configurations. In previous chapters, the importance of internal family healing was stressed, however, the complete healing process cannot be totally fulfilled without focusing on the real close relationships we encounter on a daily basis.

Healing the family involves a dynamic shuttling between our inner and outer relationship systems. This bridging between inner and outer realities can be likened to a gemologist who works with a rough diamond. Before a diamond can be fully refined, it needs to be polished on different sides, back and forth, from right to left, from the middle to the outer edges as the gemologist pays close attention to what is needed to transform the rough jewels to its innate beauty.

The therapist, like the gemologist, needs to pay close attention when to shift from one individual to another and then to the interaction between each individual. The task of the relational healer is to shuttle between the inner and outer worlds of close intimates and in this process, help to realize each individual's subparts of his/her inner family and facilitate a new integration and coherence of the relationship. In addition, the mind-body links between intimates also need to be facilitated as explained previously.

Bridging the inner and outer family involves five major stages:

1. couples/family meditation;
2. outer communication process;
3. inner family work;
4. evoking compassion;
5. grounding.

Each of these stages can take place all in one psychotherapeutic hour or over many sessions. Each stage will be described and a clinical case of a couple whose names we will call Don and Holly will be intertwined between the descriptions of the stages.

Don, 40, and Holly, 30, have been married for eight years. Don was married previously, and this is Holly's first marriage. They constantly have arguments, and their main pattern is that Don dictates and blames while Holly placates herself. Underneath Don's blaming style is an inner depressed, deprived, sad child who feels entitled to get his needs met. Holly also has an abandoned subpart, however, she has learned to suppress this part and plays out a caretaker part that reflects her role in her family of origin.

COUPLES AND FAMILY MEDITATION

Many times, it is useful to guide the couple or family through a meditative process to help disidentify people from subpersonalities and/or external roles that they play out with one another. It can also be viewed as a therapeutic ritual that can help a meaningful process to get started. When a couple or family is able to "center" themselves without attachments to inner images or outer expectations of each other, they potentially have the opportunity to really see, hear, and feel each other, sometimes for the first time. When people who are closely and emotionally connected meditate together, the potential for intimacy is increased. Many couples and/or families who have the experience of meditation for the first time have powerful spiritual openings where tremendous love, understanding, and feelings of unity infuse their consciousness.

I usually introduce meditation procedures after I have explored the couple's and/or family's relationships, presenting problems, and history as well as establishing some therapeutic goals. This enables them to get to know me so there can be increased trust as we engage in therapeutic activity that may be foreign. It is also important to note that some people have an extremely negative reaction to meditation and therefore the therapist should not push this procedure where there is great resistance. Sometimes, it is best to label this procedure as relaxation.

The following is a standard couples' meditation that I often utilize to begin sessions. The couple is instructed to sit in separate chairs as they face one another in order for them to be exactly eye level with each other. I then guide them in the following meditation:

> Allow yourselves to gently close your eyes and become aware of how you are sitting. If you need to change your position to relax yourself, allow yourself to do that now. Become aware of your breathing in and out of your nostrils. Put your full attention on the air moving in and out of your nose. If you have any difficulty concentrating, breathe a little harder through your nose and come back to that one point where the air moves in and out of your nostrils. Take a deep breath through your nose quickly, hold it, and let it go through your mouth (repeat two more times). For a moment allow yourself while you are focusing on your breathing to acknowledge your special relationship that you have with each other; the ups and downs you have experienced together, the commitment you have had up to this moment in time in being with each other. Acknowledge the special bond you have with one another. Allow yourself to keep focusing on your breathing, the air moving in and out of your nose as you slowly open up your eyes and look at each other without talking. Keep being aware of your breathing. Just experience what is happening inside of you when you look at each other. When either one of you is ready to share what you are experiencing at this moment when you look deeply into each other's eyes, allow yourself to share it with your partner.

It is important to keep the couple focused in the here and now to facilitate honest sharing from a genuine heartful place inside. In addition, it is important to allow each partner to express both negative as well as positive feelings, however, encouragement is given to whatever is spontaneously emerging in the moment.

Therapist: Why don't we go inside and center ourselves and focus on our breathing? Now, what I would like you to do is for both of you to face one another, and I want you to look into each other's eyes and breathe, and be aware of what you're feeling, what thoughts come up as you look into each other's eyes, and also to give appreciation for the time that you have been together up until now. And, while you're looking at your partner, tap into yourself while you're looking into the other's eyes and see what needs to happen in this relationship that will allow more harmony to manifest itself. And then, why don't you just share that with one another, what you're experiencing right now.

Don: For me she seems very soft; I was aware that what I had to do was not to put pressure on her; I don't want to take advantage of her . . . something I want to do is to really appreciate this moment.

Therapist: What is it that you want to be able to accomplish?

Don: I want to be able to not put her down, to control her. I have the feeling that that's what I want to do, just to accept her softness . . . my softness also.

Therapist: Can you just give to Holly a kind of statement about how much you appreciate her softness?

Don: I admire your softness, it's like . . . it's a very encompassing feeling for me, your softness . . .

Therapist: Don, what are you experiencing right now, as you say that?

Don: I feel my heart open.

As a client opens up emotionally, the inner chakra also changes. The therapist can sensitively track these changes in the body to deepen the healing work. Don is encouraged to focus on his heart center, which helps to speed up his own ability to feel his softness.

Therapist: Okay, now focus on your heart. Take a deep breath. Talk from your heart right now.

Don: I feel really happy.

Therapist: See if you can allow the happiness just to be there; take a deep breath and talk from your heart. Give it a voice, and express it.

Don: I feel a great love. I feel safe. Like you're not going to hurt me.

Therapist: What are you experiencing, Holly?

Holly: I feel open (both Holly and Don are eye gazing which is very bonding).

Therapist: What's it like to be open; tell Don.

Holly: I feel you are really with me and that you care about me and will listen to me.

A second variation of the above couple's meditation exercise comes from the Tantra Yoga tradition, where partners face each other holding hands and with their eyes open focus on their breathing, however, the task is to have the couple coordinate their breathing with each other, so when one is inhaling the other exhales. This exercise is a very powerful bonding procedure that can either be used at the beginning of a therapeutic session or after one or both partners have done individual emotional release work.

One can also do meditation in a family group circle. You instruct the family to hold each other's hands, while they close their eyes and focus on their breathing. Sometimes, I as the therapist also join in the circle as part of the therapeutic ritual. The following is an exercise that is a variation of the first one I described. This can also be adapted to use with a couple.

Everyone close their eyes as we all hold hands. Focus on your breathing in and out of your nostrils. Take a deep breath through your nose quickly and let it out slowly through your mouth (repeat two more times). Listen to my words as you focus on your breathing. We are brought here today for a special purpose. You are all connected to each other by the same blood. The relationships in the family are unique and all of you have a very special connection with each other that cannot be duplicated in the same exact way. Acknowledge for a moment that special connection as you continue to focus on your breathing in and out of your nose. What needs to happen here today? What does this family need to heal? What qualities need to be expressed in this family? What do each of you want the others to really know about you? How can you better cooperate with each other? As you continue to focus on your breathing, slowly open your eyes and look at each family member directly in their eyes. What do you experience? Get in touch with what you would like to share with each other that would aid toward the goal of healing.

The above meditation exercises are preludes to the next stage of communication where people are encouraged to talk openly, directly, and honestly with one another in a way that promotes greater understanding of each individual as well as facilitate an atmosphere of problem solving.

COMMUNICATION PROCESS

Meditational exercises are a wonderful prelude to healthy communication. Effective communication is when one is not "caught" or reacting from a subpart or role. One is able to be congruent in thinking, feeling, and action. There is no contradiction between what and how one says something. One can be honest and genuine with expressing needs and simultaneously respect the needs and wants of others. Virginia Satir called this type of communication "leveling." The following descriptions of what is done in the communication process work reflects a great many ideas of Virginia Satir's early writings. If the reader is not familiar with her books entitled *Peoplemaking* and *Conjoint Family Therapy*, you are encouraged to explore these original works.

During this stage of healing the inner and outer family, individuals face one another and continue to talk openly and directly, taking responsibility for their own positions. Individuals learn to listen to each other by using communication checks by repeating back what they heard their partner saying. If they were not received properly, the messages being sent are repeated again until the message is heard correctly.

Family members are encouraged to clarify communication that is confusing or not clear in order to refine the understanding of messages that are being sent. In addition, if any family member feels an incongruence between the content of the message and how the message was being sent, they are taught how to receive greater clarification of these nonverbal messages.

Couples and families learn how to phrase requests rather than demanding or automatically expecting things from their intimates. This stage helps individuals to acknowledge and respect differences as well as to learn how to make compromises so all parties feel heard and respected.

During the communication stage when either positive or negative emotions come up, they are encouraged to be expressed by taking responsibility with making "I" statements such as "I appreciate it when you . . . ," or "I resent . . . ," etc. When subparts emerge, the therapist helps to show the clients their internal patterns and if possible helps them get back on track.

This next section focuses on the outer communication of Don and Holly after they meditated. As communication proceeds, Don's pain emerges as he gets identified with his inner victim child subpersonality who feels persecuted by his inner controlling father, who he perceives in his wife. This part of the communication enters into Stage 3 of bridging the inner and outer family.

In this segment, Holly experiences the pain of Don usually not listening to her needs.

Holly: I am upset with him because for the last four weeks he's known that I wanted to go down to the ocean because for me it's very relaxing and I enjoy that type of thing. And for Don he likes to go down to the airport and watch the planes take off and land. That's his thing.

Well, anyway, Don's been promising me and promising me and promising me and we never go and I got upset because he said he wanted to go with his friend to go look at boats. I said, "Well fine, then forget it because you guys are going to be gone for two hours." That's their normal thing. They go and they're gone for a couple of hours and we just wouldn't have time and I got upset because I felt I was being put on the back burner and he was taking care of his things that he wanted to do and he has known for a while that I wanted to go to the ocean and it just seems like we never found the time to do what I wanted to do.

Therapist: Well, have you communicated that to him?

Holly: Yeah, I told him. I was mad.

Therapist: So what did he say about that?

Holly: He said that we would go but it was late in the afternoon.

Therapist: So did you go?

Holly: Well, we went and it was freezing cold. So we came back home.

Therapist: So what would you like Don to know about all of this with you and your needs? Talk with him.

Holly: (Holly talks directly to Don.) I'd like to have my needs fulfilled just like you get yours fulfilled. I don't put your needs on the back burner. I don't want mine put on the back burner.

Therapist: So what do you think about that? Holly's telling you that you're focused more on your wants around things that you like to do for leisure time and that you don't give her back something for her that she wants. Do you think that's true?

Don: Yeah, probably.

Therapist: Okay. What do you sense is the right kind of relationship here?

Don: It should be 50/50. I know it should be split up but somehow it doesn't work out like this.

Therapist: It seems your views are pretty clear, Holly, that you want equal distribution and Don acknowledges that.

Holly: Yes, and I don't want to remind Don about his chores (angry-critical tone).

Therapist: Now, what is your view of that, Don?

Don: Yeah. I want to help.

Therapist: Do you think it's fair for her to have to remind you of your responsibilities?

Don: No. Well, I'm pissed off (extreme anger) right now so I don't know where I'm at.

INNER FAMILY WORK

During the previous communication stage, many strong emotions can be aroused that take one away from leveling with our intimates. Certain issues that are brought up trigger deep wounds that are more rooted in the past. Oftentimes, the manner in which a message is being sent sets off extreme emotional pain. If any extreme reaction occurs and the communication is no longer able to continue without a great deal of disruption, one could suspect that subpersonalities are being activated, which points to a need for deeper exploration of one's inner family.

As a family member gets attached to one of his/her subpersonalities, the therapist immediately tunes into that person and tracks what emerging sensations are surfacing in the body as well as utilizing meditation and guided imagery procedures, as previously described.

Many times when one is doing individual internal family work, other families' pain emerges. It is important as one individual member's process finishes and another member's gets activated, the therapist will follow the next emerging wave of pain. In healing the inner and outer family work, one often oscillates from one individual to another and then facilitates dialogues between the individuals who were dealing with their pain as well as family members who were observing.

The above process was described by Virginia Satir (1988, personal communication) as constantly watching the family's contextual field and observing what "bubbles" to the surface and then activate that which stands out most in that context. The most important element in healing work according to Satir is moving toward where the most pain is in the system at any given moment.

Therapist: What are you so angry about?

Don: I don't know, I'm feeling picked on.

Therapist: You often get hurt when you feel accused of, especially, something you didn't do.

Don: Yeah, something I didn't do, because that happened a lot when I was a kid. Everything that went wrong, it was my fault.

Therapist: What are you aware of right now when you talk about this inside yourself?

Don: Just instances when I was a kid of things that happened that I had no control over and I got blamed for it.

Therapist: What circumstances are coming up now?

Don: Probably my dad. One of the drivers had come into the yard and parked the truck in the wrong place and the next morning I was the first one there and he . . . my father came into the shop and instantly . . . "You little asshole, I told you about parking trucks there." I didn't park it there, and he just like climbed right down my throat. I was all of thirteen years old.

Therapist: And what did you do?

Don: I just said, "I don't need this" and turned around and walked away.

Therapist: You didn't say anything?
Don: I didn't say a word. I didn't get mad. I mean I got mad inside, but I didn't let it out.
Therapist: Well, I wonder, you know . . . maybe we should work with this a little bit. Because it comes up . . . it comes up in both of you. Do you want to do that?
Don: I guess. I've got no choice.

The next segment begins inner family work via guided imagery of internal adolescent and father. The client is prepared to enter into this work while centering on his breathing.

Therapist: Well, you've been through this before so . . . why don't you go inside and just take some deep breaths and just focus right now. Imagine yourself in a situation, thirteen years old with your dad. Do you see an image of yourself? Okay, what do you look like?
Don: Good-looking little kid. Skinny but cute.
Therapist: Can you see the image of your dad?
Don: Oh, yeah.
Therapist: What does he look like?
Don: Big, mean, and ugly.
Therapist: Okay, I want you to kind of identify with that thirteen-year-old image, and I want you to express out what you're feeling towards Dad right now.
Don: Just anger and hate.
Therapist: Okay, express that. "I hate you, Dad."
Don: "I hate you, Dad."
Therapist: Let the anger come out and tell him what you're so angry about.
Don: "I'm angry because you never let me say what . . . you never let me express my feelings. You always accuse, accuse, accuse. You never listen to my side. Never. Neither one of you ever did."
Therapist: Okay, what are you experiencing now, Don, inside your body?
Don: It's real strange. I want to get angry but I'm not. I don't feel bad about not being angry.
Therapist: Okay, see if you can say, "Dad, I feel strange talking to you this way."

Don: "I feel strange talking to you like this, Dad. It's a new experience."

Therapist: Okay, tell him what that's like to just talk to him this way.

Don: "It's different."

Therapist: Express to him how it's different.

Don: "I get to speak. I don't have to stand there and be accused of doing something that I didn't do."

Therapist: Tell him what it feels like for you now to speak out.

Don: "It feels good."

Therapist: Tell him what you wished he would have done with you.

Don: "Listened. Listened to me once in a while. I wasn't perfect, and I could do things on my own."

Therapist: Tell him one of the things you could have done on your own or that you did do.

Don: "Worked my ass off for you, busting them fucking tires, taking care of that whiny truck driver you had, cleaning up, loading trailers by myself, listening to you and Mother piss and moan about the stupidest things."

Therapist: What are you experiencing now?

Don: I don't know . . . maybe sorrow they never could see that. We might have gotten along a lot better.

Therapist: Express that to Dad.

Don: "Dad, I wish you would have seen my good points."

The therapist needs to continue to track the emerging affect of Don and mirror back his feeling states as well as encouraging him to express his pain toward his internal father.

During this next segment, one can see the clear emotional patterns connected to earlier emotional pain with the father and how these reactions are repeated with his wife.

Therapist: Tell him what that would have meant to you.

Don: "It would have meant maybe you loved me."

Therapist: Can you tell him what you're feeling right now? You look pretty sad. Can you tell Dad what your sadness is about?

Don: "You just never paid any attention. You're always so wrapped up in the bottle and all the things that didn't mean anything. You

couldn't see the things that meant something. You couldn't see me for what I was."
Therapist: Tell Dad how this has affected your life.
Don: "It screwed me up."
Therapist: Tell him how it screwed you up.
Don: "Every time somebody accuses me of something that I know I didn't do, I get mad. I get angry. I'm always on the defensive. I'm afraid to tell people what I really think."
Therapist: Okay, see your dad. Tell your dad what you really think about this whole situation.
Don: "I really think you're an asshole."
Therapist: What are you aware of right now inside?
Don: Sorrow and anger.
Therapist: What's the strongest?
Don: Sorrow.

It is important for the therapist to track the most dominant of affective states. It is often the case that before anger and rage can be experienced, one has to embrace one's sorrow.

In the segment that follows Don grieves his father for the first time in his life which triggers anger that is also encouraged to be released.

Therapist: Just express the sadness. Tell Dad the longing you had maybe, for him, about what you really needed from him.
Don: "I needed understanding. I needed some time together–father and son time. I needed advice that I could never get from you."
Therapist: Tell him what kind of advice you wished you could have got from him.
Don: "Life, what it's really about. How the world is not all bad."
Therapist: Okay, what are you experiencing now, Don, as you talk?
Don: I wish he was here. (His father is dead.)
Therapist: Tell him that.
Don: "I wish you were here right now."
Therapist: Tell him why that would be important to you.
Don: "I'd like to tell you everything I just said right to your face."
Therapist: Tell him why that would be so important to you.

Don: "I could finally stand up to you. Maybe try and make you understand what I feel, that I wasn't your little puppy dog you could order around and if your day went shitty you wouldn't come home and blame it on me."

The client releases some grief over loss of father's approval which activates his rage. It is important that the therapist acts as the magnifier and amplifier of intensifying affective states. In this next segment the therapist plays the role of the client's critical father in order to trigger greater emotional release in the clients.

Therapist: Okay, Don. Take some deep breaths right now. What I want you to do, even though he's not . . . he's gone right now . . . what I want you to do is I want you to stand up to him right now and think of the situations and what you would really have wanted to say when he would have . . . . What is the first situation that pops into your mind?

Don: God, there are hundreds of them . . . no, millions.

Therapist: Just, what is the first thing that pops into your mind? What's happening now?

Don: I can't slow them down. They're just going by so fast I can't focus on one.

Therapist: What did your father used to say to you that really got to you? (Going after the pain.)

Don: He used to call me an asshole about twenty-five times a day.

Therapist: Okay. Alright. I'm going to take the role of your father, Don, and stay with that child inside of you. I'm going to be that critical father. I want you to respond back. "Don, you're an asshole."

Don: "So are you. Why do you keep calling me an asshole? I don't need this."

Therapist: Tell him what you really think about him.

Don: "You're an asshole. You won't listen to anybody. You're going to do it your own way no matter what. You're stubborn, you're a drunk."

Therapist: Stand up to him like you would really want to. Tell him exactly what you want him to hear. Something like, "Get off my back?" Let it out. What is it? What do you really want to say to him? If you can put it into words, what would you want to say to him?

Don: "Just leave me alone. Leave me alone."

Therapist: Say that again. Say it louder. As loud as you can go.
Don: "LEAVE ME ALONE!"
Therapist: "Dad, leave me alone." Express it fully out, Don. What's happening inside?
Don: I just can't let go. I'm afraid to let go.
Therapist: Afraid to let go? We've been here before, haven't we? What are you afraid of right now?
Don: Myself.
Therapist: What are you afraid is going to happen if you let go?
Don: I don't know.
Therapist: What is it? What do you feel like doing to Dad?
Don: Beating the shit out of him, or trying anyway.

In the next segment, the therapist encourages the full release of his rage by getting the client to get on his knees and beat pillows with his fists while expressing his pent-up aggression that he never allowed himself to directly experience. Then, the client once again goes into further grieving that gets released after he is able to get unburdened with the expression of anger.

Therapist: Put your fists together like this and pound the pillow. "I hate you, Dad." Blurt it out.
Don: "I hate you."
Therapist: Take some breaths. "I hate you."
Don: "I hate you."
Therapist: Pound it.
Don: "I hate you. I hate you. I HATE YOU. I HATE YOU . . . I HATE YOU for what you've done to me" (starts to weep profusely).
Therapist: Okay, just stay with that a minute. Stay with it. Just stay with that grief, Don. It's been there for a long time. (Don cries for 10-15 minutes while Holly also starts to grieve watching the intensity of her husband's pain.) What's going on inside right now, Don?
Don: I'm deeply sad.
Therapist: There's a lot of sadness there, isn't there? About all those years you had to put up with that, huh? Why don't you sit back on the couch? Take some deep breaths. What are you experiencing inside of you right now? (Tracking the body's energy field)
Don: Relief!

In this segment, the client experiences a deep relief in his body. He is encouraged to fully experience the emerging sensations in his body as he allows himself to feel a deep connection to himself. Once again, he goes into his chest, which is the seat of love and compassion where he experiences a great deal of peace.

This calmness is amplified through meditation. The open heart center in this deeply relaxed state is facilitated to help the early child image by putting this image into the chest area of the body. Transpersonal imagery is utilized with the sun moving through the upper chakras to the chest to ground this experience.

Therapist: Okay, where inside your body do you experience the relief?

Don: In the chest.

Therapist: Okay, good. Focus right on your chest right now. Focus right on your chest–in the center of your chest–all your attention and take some deep breaths and focus right in the center of your chest. What are you experiencing?

Don: A calmness.

Therapist: A calmness. Okay. What I want you to do is go deeper into that calmness. Focus on the calmness in your heart. Now, what is going on in your heart now? What are you experiencing now?

Don: A calmness I don't think I've ever felt. (A deep letting go in the body that is very healing which can be facilitated into a meditation)

Therapist: Okay, just let that calmness in. See it as a gift right now. Just really let that calmness in. And give words to the calmness in your heart. I am calm . . . (using affirmation can open up the inner experience more).

Don: I am calm.

Therapist: I am the center of calmness.

Don: I am the center of calmness.

Therapist: Keep talking from your heart from this calmness. Just let it come out, about the relief that you're feeling and the calmness right now.

Don: I am calm. I am relaxed. I don't feel any pressure.

Therapist: I'm without pressure.

Don: I'm without pressure. I feel relief.

Therapist: Take some deep breaths and go deeper into your heart right now. What sensations are around your heart right now?

Don: A deep calmness.

Therapist: Alright, just stay with the calmness right now. Stay with that calm feeling. I want you to see that little child inside of you, the one that's been hurt by Dad and Mom. See that child? (Using heart chakra and meditation to heal inner child image, this can be facilitated by the transpersonal symbol like the sun. The next segment shows how to do this.)

Don: Uh-huh.

Therapist: Okay, I want you to put that child right in your heart right now. What I want you to do, Don, is to imagine a sun overhead, a bright sun that is right directly on top of your head with that child inside your heart right now. See the sun? Okay, I want you to let in the light of the sun, the brilliant light of the sun slowly come into your heart and beam down on that child that's been really hurt deeply. Bring that sun's light right into that child, into the center of your heart and as you do that, what's happening to that child?

Don: He's warm.

Therapist: Okay. Stay with that. Stay with that warmth now that you're experiencing. Explain the warmth to me that you're experiencing right now. How does it feel to have that warmth around your heart, around the child?

Don: Good.

Therapist: Let that light kind of help heal the wounds of that child right now. Let it circulate all throughout that child's body, directly in the center of your heart. What's happening to the energy of the child when you allow that to happen?

Don: It's just . . . I can see him but I don't know where he's standing. He's just looking up.

Therapist: Okay. Can you let him look up at you right now? Can you imagine him looking up to you right now? Can you see that?

Don: Uh-huh. I am holding him in my chest. I love him (Don cries).

Therapist: Okay, Don, now what I want you to do is just take some deep breaths. Just acknowledge that you . . . what you've experienced right now and when you're ready just come back to the room, just reassuring that child that you're not going to abandon him. You're just going to leave him just for now.

EVOKING COMPASSION

As individual family members work with healing their own inner family through deep emotional release work, there is a natural tendency for others in the family to feel connected or reconnected to one another in a profound bonding manner. Other close intimates experienced their bodies opening up, too. As family members experience each other's suffering, especially the pain that has been accumulated and handed down through previous generational struggles, the quality of deep compassion is evoked.

When compassion becomes fully experienced in the family's emotional field, other higher qualities can infuse all the members such as greater understanding, love, and forgiveness. The deepest healing work that can occur as compassion permeates the family collective is that of current generations exonerating previous generations. Boszormenyi-Nagy and Krasner (1986), pioneers of family therapy and founders of contextual family therapy, clearly attribute the difference between exoneration and forgiveness, and their relationship to healing relationships. They state:

> Exoneration is a process of lifting the load of culpability off the shoulders of a given person whom heretofore we may have blamed. In our experience, clinical improvement often coincides with the renewed capacity of parents to exonerate their own seemingly failing parents. (p. 416)

> Exoneration differs from forgiveness. The act of forgiveness usually *retains* the assumption of guilt and extends the forgiver's generosity to the person who has injured her or him. Offering forgiveness, a person now refrains from holding the culprit accountable and from demanding punishment. In contrast, exoneration typically results from an adult's reassessment of the failing parent's own past childhood victimization. It replaces the framework of blame with mature appreciation of a given person's or situation's past options, efforts, and limits. (p. 416)

The next part of this is getting Holly to respond to Don's work. She has been visibly deeply touched as she has observed his process. This helps to ground the individual work of Don's and then bridges it with the relationship. Couples meditation is utilized to help unite them and open their hearts.

Utilizing couples meditation helps the couple unify energetically at a nonverbal level. Unification is at the heart of healing in couples and family work. Often individuals that have relationship difficulties were deeply wounded as children and in deep relationship healing work, the couple can utilize their own relationship to fix the original hurt and pain by bonding with each other after strong emotional release is accomplished.

Therapist: (To Holly) What are you experiencing right now? Through all this, what were you experiencing?
Holly: Just relief. Relief for Don.
Therapist: Can you relate to any of this?
Holly: Yeah, I can.
Therapist: Tell Don how you can relate to it.
Holly: I know how your hatred feels because I've felt that way a lot towards my mom. I wish she hadn't done what she did. We just have to acknowledge it and go on with our lives so we can be free. Through your work, it helps me to let go of my resentments toward my parents seeing that they couldn't do anything more than they could do; they were victim to their own parent suffering.
Therapist: What are you feeling towards Don right now?
Holly: Lots of love. I don't feel sorry for Don. I feel empathy.
Therapist: How does it feel to feel empathy for Don?
Holly: A bond, a tie, a connection.
Therapist: How do you take that, Don?
Don: I feel very close to Holly.
Therapist: You do? Okay, tell her.
Don: I feel very close to you, closer all the time.
Therapist: Tell her how it is, getting closer.
Don: Like you're part of me. Like we're just kind of joining together. Understanding each other's faults. How we think. Bonding. Something we haven't had before, I don't think. Superficial maybe, but nothing deep.

In this next segment, the therapist facilitates a unification experience through long eye gazing which is very powerful practice for connecting deeply. The therapist also encourages physical touching and holding to further ground this bonding.

Therapist: Why don't you just look at each other and take some deep breaths right now. Focus on your breaths. Just feel that connection right here now. Just really acknowledge how you guys are working in this relationship and trying to understand each other and deepening that bond with each other. Gaze at each other's eyes as you heal each other and your relationship.

GROUNDING

The last stage of healing the inner and outer family is for members to reengage in ongoing dialogue about how the individual's internal family world has affected the here and now transaction and what everyone would be willing to do to promote greater trustworthiness in the future. This would include conversation about working out perceived injustices as well as reestablishing the fair balance of giving and taking in their relationship.

Ivan Boszormenyi-Nagy (1987) in his work in contextual therapy discusses the importance of this ongoing need to balance and rebalance the give and take between close intimates in order for there to be evolutionary relational progress into subsequent generations. He calls this process "transgenerational solidarity." Boszormenyi-Nagy states:

> All that can be expected of humans is a periodic monitoring of consequences from both the self's and other's vantage point . . . One form of caring about posterity consists of caring to review and revise the legacy expectation of the past for the benefit of the future. (p. 313)

The couple/family continues to discuss real things that they want to see changed and now they are more open to compromising and making new agreements and relational contracts with one another.

Therapist: Now, that you both have worked very deeply with each other, what do you think you could do now to further help out this relationship?

Holly: I have a greater understanding of how big Don's wound is when he was young. I never realized how abused he was as a child. I feel I have to be careful not to use a harsh accusing tone in my voice. But, I also need to put out my needs and not just be Don's caretaker.

Therapist: Talk with Don about that now.

Holly: I see now that I need to speak with you in a tone that won't call up your past hurts. However, I also realize I have to stop being a caretaker to your little hurt boy. I have needs of my own and I want you to listen to them.

Don: I know you do. I have to stop thinking that the world owes me and realize I have to give some, too. It would be helpful if you put your needs out to me in a less critical way. I will be able to hear you better.

Holly: Yes, I will try as long as you acknowledge my needs and give to me on my terms without a negative attitude.

Don: Okay, I will try too. I appreciate you being here with me (starts to cry). I feel sensitive right now letting you see how I hurt so much.

Holly: (Goes over and hugs Don) I like when we can connect deeply like this. I respect you for allowing yourself to hurt. I do too!

The above process of bridging inner and outer family healing can be done with an individual, couple, and/or family. The flexible applications have many permutations, however, the important principle as was stated in the beginning of this chapter is to allow shuttling between the individual's internal world to outer family healing processes. The essence of the process is to increase compassion, love, and forgiveness which is at the apex of spiritual qualities between oneself and other family members. As a latency aged, adolescent, or adult child observes his parents' internal healing, greater bonding occurs which opens more respectful congruent communication. This will be demonstrated in Chapter 13.

The inner family healing processes can also be done when three or more generations are in the same room. For example, it is quite awesome to experience a grandparent or great-grandparent engage in the inner family process as subsequent generations watch with incredible intent as ancestral links unfold before everyone's eyes.

Chapter 13

Bridging the Inner and Outer Family of Origin

In Chapters 8 through 11, I discussed the power of healing the intragenerational family through meditation and guided imagery. As we are able to synthesize the variety of intragenerational splits, we are infused with an increase of psychospiritual emotional energy states from the supraconscious including understanding, compassion, love, forgiveness, joy, and unity.

Sometimes working with integrating the intragenerational images can be a preparation for grounding this work within family of origin sessions. Family of origin sessions involve working with the active, real, original family including siblings and parents. At times, this can be done with one's grandparents if they are alive. During family of origin sessions one can ground the previous internal intragenerational work by resolving historical and present ongoing interactions with one's real family.

Jim Framo (1982), pioneer of family of origin therapy states:

> The client by having sessions with his or her family of origin, takes the problems back to where they began, thereby making available a direct route to etiological functions. Dealing with real, external parental figures is designed to loosen the grip of the internal representation of these figures and expose them to reality considerations . . . . (p. 173, *Explorations in Marital and Family Therapy*)

Framo (1992) also states the core importance of family of origin work:

... in family of origin sessions, past bitterness toward parents and siblings can be dissipated and mothers and fathers can be perceived as real people . . . you have the opportunity to come to terms with parents before they die. (pp. 2, 3)

Family of origin therapy is a well-developed approach, and I encourage the reader to explore an updated comprehensive volume by James L. Framo (1992) entitled *Family of Origin Therapy: An Intergenerational Approach*, Brunner/Mazel, New York.

Framo's main method is to have clients formulate an agenda that they will investigate together with their family of origin. Framo's main role in the session is one of facilitation to have family members discuss pertinent issues directly with one another in a straightforward, honest, open manner. Through dialogue emerges healing interactions. These healing encounters often come as a result of the parents recounting their history with their parents. As one's siblings or aging parents come in contact with past pains, hurts, and frustrations with their own parents, the adult child is able to empathize with other family members in a different manner than he previously has been able.

In my work with bridging the inner and outer family of origin, my approach differs from Framo's in the way in which I enter into the historical material that gets told by the older generations. Instead of merely facilitating a deep meaningful conversation, I have different family members including siblings, parents, or grandparents engage in healing their intragenerational family through meditation and guided imagery. The younger generation has an opportunity to witness their own siblings or parents working on their own struggles experientially. As an adult child witnesses his or her own sibling or parent shuttling through an intragenerational experience, the heart is increasingly infused with a deep profound sense of understanding compassion, love, and forgiveness. The previous intragenerational healing sessions often mirror the real intergenerational encounters. The new bond that can occur between the siblings or next generation is awesome, and the family's spirit is reconnected. This reconnection or unification is the hallmark of the spiritual dimension in family healing.

The following are excerpts from a clinical transcript entitled "The Ghost of Father Revisited Through Siblings." Present in the session is Coleen who organized this meeting with brother Ron, sister Sheryl, and her mother, Florence.

There are many themes that are worked on in the family, however, the segment that follows focuses on the distant relationship between brother and sister. Each sibling reacts negatively to the other out of painfully perceiving the negative aspects of their deceased father in one another.

FAMILY MEDITATION

Just as in a couples meditation where two individuals are "centering" themselves in their internal space that is not identified with any subpart or roles for the purpose of achieving an I-Thou relationship to begin to do healing work, family meditation aims for exactly the same goal.

Positive synergy is created when the therapist assesses the individual and family's collective will toward accomplishing emerging goals for everyone's next step in their growth process.

As a therapist gathers up information about what is imbalanced in the system from family members, he reflects back to the family's higher spiritual qualities that are needed to create increased family harmony. A family meditation is facilitated to open each member up to the painful work that needs to be done before the positive qualities can emerge.

Family meditational processes can be also viewed as a therapeutic ritual to begin and end an intensive emotional process.

The following is an example of the therapist facilitating a family meditative ritual that comes after the family discussed what their goals were for the session.

Therapist: I'd like to do a ritual. Maybe we could all hold hands. Okay, feel kind of connected together, as we all are today. And see if you can just close your eyes. . . . (Pause.) And what I want you to do is to take some deep breaths, and the best way for you to do that is to take your breath quickly through your nose and slowly let it out through your mouth. . . . (Pause.) Then focus on your breathing, realizing that your breath gives you life. And think about everything that you've all said and the things you've heard from one another and about what is trying to emerge in this family right now. I've heard there needs to be a deeper understanding for each other today, and a deeper connection, which will bring more love. There needs to be support and recognition and acknowledgment and less sense of being separated. So just acknowledge what everybody just said and what came out right now about moving towards those kind of qualities for the rest of today . . . and if anything comes up that must be hard to talk about, or hurtful and painful, let there just be an acknowledgment for that to be here as a necessary variable to help in healing wounds that are inside each of you. Okay, whoever would like to talk.

EMBRACING FAMILY PAIN

After a family meditation there is generally a more open atmosphere to explore painful emotions. The emerging pain points to a direction to work within the inner or outer family dimension. The skilled therapist follows the natural waves of pain. For example, as an individual becomes tense, withdrawn, constricted, increases or decreases breathing rate, and/or begins to manifest a visible emotion like sadness through tears watering up in the eye, the therapist watches the other family members' potential pain and sees where therapeutic attention needs to be placed.

This next excerpt opens with a great deal of emotional woundedness between Coleen and her brother, Ron.

Toward the end of this segment, Ron realizes that his sister reminds him of his unfinished business with his father.

Coleen: I've been trying to figure my life out for a lot of years and trying to just heal and survive. I just don't think any of you really have a conception of . . . what's that grin about? (laughs)
Ron: You came out right, after all! (brother and sister laugh) And I love you, Coleen.
Coleen: (Crying) You say that, but I don't believe you.
Ron: I do, honey.
Coleen: What's the evidence? You don't see me, you don't call me, you don't . . . you're not nice to me when I come to see you. . . you don't understand . . . I ask you to make a stupid phone call and you dump shit on me. You know, that hurts.

Therapist: I think that the important thing here is that something is unclear about your relationship. There's miscommunication. What is your sense about that, Ron? What is the estrangement between you two?

Ron: I don't know . . . I think maybe . . . maybe probably it's some of the same relationship that I had with my dad. I saw him pursuing his own self-centered goals. I was being expected to jump to whatever he said. And forget anything else that I might want to do. And, maybe I'm seeing the same thing with my sister. I'm really in need of something and . . . and I'm being asked to take part in that again . . . somehow like a broken record that . . . my dad and now my sister wants me to do things but doesn't give me what I need.

OUTER AND INNER SHUTTLING

In family sessions, the therapist tracks for the timing of transitions between outer transactions and inner intragenerational work. When a clear wave of pain is amplified and becomes manifested in the fore-front in the transaction, the therapist facilitates the focus on the individual's emerging affect and where it is occurring in the body. This often is a gateway to the intragenerational work.

In this next section, the therapist shuttles from the outer relationship between Ron and his sister Coleen to Ron's internal process and works with parts of his inner family. The therapist focuses Ron on the emerging sensations in his body (stomach) and facilitates a guided imagery experience with his father, Tom, in order to deal with expressing his grief and resentments, which is part of the healing process.

Therapist: When you talk about your father and Coleen what are you experiencing inside?

Ron: I get . . . sort of . . . kind of tight; I feel kind of tense in my stomach. I am in pain about my father.

Therapist: Why don't you close your eyes and see an image of Dad and talk with him. Could you tell, just imagine that you're going to talk to Dad from that kind of hurt child inside as if he were here listening— he can't be here. But tell him what you have wished, what you wished that you could have gotten from him when you were young as if he was here. How would you call him, Papa or Dad or? . . . (Ron closes eyes and images his father.)

Ron: I don't know . . . I called him Tom. That was his first name.

Therapist: Okay. Tell Tom what you really wanted from him when you were small. I know it is going to be hard. (There's a long silence in which Ron takes deep breaths and the therapist encourages him by saying, "Let it out." Ron is also crying.) Talk to your dad about your sadness right now. His spirit is here with us.

Ron: I wish we had played together. You made some real efforts to do that because you knew there was some hurt going on. (Crying hard) I know you really tried . . . but I wish . . .

Therapist: Tell him what you wished.

Ron: I needed to see that you weren't perfect. I needed to see that you made mistakes.

Therapist: Tell him why you needed that.

Ron: I had (told my mother) I couldn't live up to his expectation.

Therapist: "I couldn't live up to your expectations, Dad."

Ron: "Dad, I'm sorry I couldn't be all you wanted me to be" . . . I feel pretty good about the fact that I got to say a word or two before he died. I, ah . . . I do feel bad that I didn't get a chance to be with him on the farm. I didn't feel like I was given a chance. I think I had sort of built up resentments that I . . . he wouldn't play with me. He was too involved with himself. I tried to please him.

In this next section, the therapist shuttles back from Ron's internal process to the inner feelings of Coleen. The reason this was done at this moment was because Coleen visibly shows some pain. As pain emerges nonverbally in her face, the therapist continues to activate that individual and helps to bridge the outer relationship in some kind of dialogue. This helps to balance out the healing of the inner and outer family process. In this case, when the pain is able to be experienced and let go, family members can begin to negotiate a different kind of relationship in the future.

Therapist: (To brother) I have a feeling you're not the only one in this family who has got sadness about your dad. . . . Coleen, do you want to say anything to your brother?

Coleen: Yeah, I feel like (her voice gets very low) we sort of have identical experiences.

Therapist: How are you feeling towards Ron now?

Coleen: I really feel stupid . . . I feel close to him but I still don't feel like he feels close to me. My dad is in the way.

Therapist: (To brother) What are you experiencing right now when you look at Coleen?

Ron: (Crying) I don't know . . . it's so . . . it's just hard . . . it's . . .

Therapist: Hard to have the connection?

Ron: It's just kind of buried there.

Therapist: I see you are in a lot of pain.

Ron: (Crying hard) I'm sorry . . . my feelings are just not there.

Coleen: I'd rather you be truthful and not pretend by saying, "I love you," but you don't feel it.

Ron: I do love you, Col.

Coleen: Dad loved me too, but he never understood me. He never knew me. He just loved me because I was his daughter.

Therapist: Are you aware of the barrier right now? About this barrier between you two?

Ron: There isn't anything that I can point to. There is nothing about you that I don't like. You just remind me of Dad and there is so much pain there.

Therapist: Tell Coleen what you need from her for you to feel less of a barrier about your relationship. Tell her what you need for yourself that maybe you haven't gotten from her.

Ron: (Crying) I guess it's kind of like with Dad . . . I would like you to come over to my hangar, look at my old airplane. Maybe you will go for a ride with me that . . . just take a look at it . . . it's interesting.

Therapist: Tell her that you want her to play with you.

Ron: Yes, I would like to play and have fun with you.

BRIDGING INTRAGENERATIONAL AND FAMILY OF ORIGIN HEALING

This next long segment deals with doing intragenerational healing through guided imagery and meditation with brother Ron and his deceased father. There is also guided imagery work with Ron's inner father and grandfather. Ron appears to be carrying the grief of his father for himself as well as other family members. As he moves into the necessary internal work he is released from the fetters of the past and helps others to open up further too.

Therapist: (To Ron, brother) Close your eyes for just a minute. I want you to get an image of Dad and I want you to get an image of Dad in his vulnerable places. I want you to see him as a boy. I just want you to allow yourself to experience that and what I want you to do is also get an image of his father. I want you to identify with the image that you have of Tom as a little boy and I want you to imagine becoming that little boy (or even as a teenager) and what I want you to do is to really kind of get into his shoes right now. Keep your eyes closed and take some deep breaths.

Ron: (I am Tom and I am five.) I am very insecure. I have a good mother who is basically a housewife and takes care of me . . . but all of a sudden my father died. Before he died, he told me that I was the man of the house and it's like my childhood ended and it's just like my life is gone too.

Therapist: Tom, tell me what it was like for you. (Therapist talks to inner child of inner parent.)

Ron: "Yeah, I'm scared. I can't take the place of my father . . . I'm a kid. I'm scared. I don't know what to do."

Therapist: Let me talk to Tom inside of you. "Tom, how does it feel to take on the family responsibility?"

Ron: "I'm so scared. I'm so empty."

Therapist: Get an image of your inner grandfather and have your inner father talk to him about his emptiness.

Ron: "Mom is so weak. I'm it. My sisters can't do anything and my brother's gone, and it's just overwhelming, and I don't know what to do."

Therapist: Is there anything else that Tom wants to express to his father?

Ron: "I didn't want you to die. I didn't want you to leave us alone. I'm angry at you for dying."

Therapist: Okay, express that anger: "I'm angry with you."

Ron: (Expressing anger more emphatically) "I'M ANGRY WITH YOU! HOW DARE YOU JUST DIE AND LEAVE ME WITH ALL THIS! IT'S YOUR JOB, NOT MINE! I AIN'T GONNA FINISH YOUR JOB! I'M GOING TO BE ME, WHATEVER THAT IS, I DON'T KNOW WHAT IT IS YET! I DON'T HAVE TO ACT AS IF I'M A MAN! I'M NOT A MAN! I'M A LITTLE KID. HOW DARE YOU JUST DIE AND LEAVE ME WITH ALL THIS! "

Therapist: (Therapist has Ron continue to talk from the inner child of father to his father.) Tell your father how it was without him on the farm.

Ron: "I know I'm strong enough to do this because you said, 'Be a man,' and I'll do it. I have doubts about it but I'm not going to let it show. I will not let you down. I will be a man and take care of my sisters and . . ."

Therapist: What is it like for you inside? (Therapist talking to Ron's inner child of his father) What do you want your daddy (Ron's grandfather) to see about you inside?

Ron: Nobody sees me. Give me a chance to just be a little boy and play and be silly. (This is a repetitive intergenerational theme.)

Therapist: And what was it like not to be able to play, be silly? What was it like for you?

Ron: It pulled me away from other people, unable to be in touch with them.

Therapist: It sounds like, Tom, you were pretty lonely.

Ron: Yeah. I feel empty. (cries)

Therapist: Let those tears in. Okay, I want you to imagine right now your dad's father.

Ron: I have a picture of him.

Therapist: Okay, you have a picture of him. What I want you to imagine is that your father's father is talking to him. Tom is now empty (inside or sad). Now, have his father talk to him. Imagine Tom now as in front in you and his father is talking to him about what Tom has expressed to him. See if he can respond to Tom. Tom said he needed your love.

Ron: Yeah.

Therapist: (Therapist talks to Ron's inner grandfather) Do you see that Tom is so sad? That he wants your love? It is hard for you to give it to him?

Ron: I can't show weakness . . .

Therapist: Okay, say that to Tom: "I can't show my weakness to you."

Ron: "Tom, I can't show you my feelings" (said in a very low, gentle voice).

Therapist: What does Tom look like in your image?

Ron: So lonely!!

Therapist: How rough it must have been for your father as a little boy. (Ron is crying loudly.)

GROUNDING THE OUTER FAMILY

The next section is a time that family members can talk about rebalancing their relationship in the future. The next segment depicts this kind of dialogue between Coleen and Ron. This work is especially helpful after intragenerational dialogue when there is increased understanding, compassion, and love for close intimates.

Therapist: Okay, Ron, now I want you to go sit by your sister over there. Coleen, what do you want from Ron right now?
Coleen: I want you to know me. I don't feel you know me.
Ron: (Crying, laughing) I don't feel like you know me, either.
Coleen: I feel like I know you better than you know me (laughs).
Therapist: How do you feel right now with Ron?
Coleen: I feel like there's a chance (starts crying). There's a chance for me to make it with you, Ron. I understand your pain with Dad!
Ron: Yeah.
Therapist: Will you make a statement about what you want from now into the future?
Coleen: I want to be me with you more. I don't want to see Dad through you. I want Dad to move away. And I don't want to be your big sister either. I don't want to be any of those roles. I've been personally through a lot of pain and lots of struggles. I want to have more fun. I'd like to dance with you. (Ron laughs.) I'll dance your ass off. And I don't want you to ever, ever say I'm no fun again, ever!
Therapist: What are you experiencing right now, Ron?
Ron: (Laughs) It still feels a little awkward, but there is new beginning. I don't have to see my dad in my sister.
Therapist: Well, it is special work that you guys get to carry on. So in working on your relationship you can heal your sibling relationship as well as your relationship with your dad. So I think it is a package deal.

FORGIVENESS IN INTERGENERATIONAL HEALING

In bridging the inner and outer family of origin work, one of the most satisfying healing encounters is when real forgiveness can occur between an aging parent and an adult child. This often can occur when the adult child experiences the intensity of experiencing the parent's intragenerational healing.

In the next section, Coleen is able to relieve a great deal of pent-up anger and grief over her mother's unavailability to her in the past as well as the present. She is able to let go of resentments and open her heart to love and forgiveness. This section was preceded by Coleen's mother doing some intragenerational work. Coleen has learned through her mother's intragenerational imagery process that her maternal grandmother was very cut off from her emotional self. Thus, her mother learned to be unavailable emotionally to others.

Coleen is able to express her need to be held when she's sad and her mother fixes her past stoic emotionally uninvolved response with hugging and comforting her daughter in the here and now.

Coleen: I feel like all my life I've heard about my father's loneliness and I'm tired of it.

Therapist: Are you angry about this?

Coleen: I am tired of him being the focus, him being, his past being such a shadow on all of us forever. I feel that, Mom.

Mom: Yeah.

Coleen: I feel that all my life I suffered his pain and I don't want to suffer it anymore, not one minute more.

Mom: Oh, Colie, how can we get away from it?

Coleen: I'm determined to get away.

Therapist: What else are you angry with your mom about?

Coleen: Mom, I feel like you are Dad's wife, but you weren't our mom. Emotionally, he was always first. You were not available; you are not available now. You are still back there in Arkansas with Dad.

Mom: Right.

Coleen: And I don't want to be there anymore. I've been through a lot of hells, and I want to be here today, not tomorrow.

Therapist: Where are you?

Coleen: I'm angry that I've had to live his life. I've had to be his loneliness.

Therapist: Did Mom know any of your pain?

Coleen: Maybe, somewhat.

Therapist: My sense is that you all felt that Mom wasn't tuned in. Mom was taking care of Dad. Yeah. So tell her how you feel, what you needed (encourages direct dialogue with mother).

Coleen: I feel like you put Dad first all the time, this poor little boy that lost his father. I lost my father too, and so did Ron, and I needed more from you emotionally. You couldn't deal with sadness; you couldn't deal with my pain.

Therapist: (Therapist gets Coleen and Mother to make eye contact.) Look at her, Mom. And you too. Look at her in her eyes.

Coleen: (Crying) I don't want to hurt you, Mom, like I said.

Mom: Don't worry, dear.

In this next segment, an authentic honest dialogue between mother and daughter ensues. Coleen's early childhood longing was to be held by her mother when she was sad. During this next part of the session this experience is corrected by Coleen's mother embracing her during the session as she supports Coleen's grief.

Therapist: Tell your mom what else you needed from her, Coleen.

Coleen: I needed you to just let me hurt when I hurt. When we moved it was so painful for me, and you couldn't let me be with my pain. You couldn't just let me cry. You had to say "Don't cry, don't feel bad." And I know this was to protect you. And I protected you. I took care of you. You didn't take care of me emotionally.

Therapist: Tell Mom what you really wanted from her and everybody else.

Coleen: I wanted somebody when I was sad to just hold me and let me cry and let me talk about it, and let me be what I was feeling. And I didn't feel that I could do that. I didn't feel like I knew how to ask for that. And I didn't feel like it was okay to have that.

Therapist: What do you think about that, Mom? Have you thought about that before? Talk to your daughter about it.

Mom: I was struggling so hard all my life to get along with Dad.

Coleen: I know you were.

Mom: To combat him.

Coleen: I know it.

Therapist: Is there anything you want to say back to her about the times when she felt unprotected? .

Mom: Oh, I felt your pain so much. I needed to face things that were real back then with Dad. I couldn't do that then, but I can face them now with you.

Therapist: What's wrong, Coleen?

Coleen: (Crying) It's been nice to hear her say how she can face what's real.

Therapist: Do you feel there's a lot of that child in you who wishes Mom was there and . . .

Coleen: It's just that I wanted you to hold me and let me cry (crying).

Therapist: How about right now, Mom. It's not too late.

Mom: Oh, Coleen. (Coleen is crying as mother holds her.) I should have gotten up and gone back to you at those times when I remember you were in such pain. I shouldn't have just jumped off and gone.

Coleen: You always said, "Don't cry; it will be okay."

Mom: I didn't want you to be sad because I didn't want you to be hurt.

Coleen: I know, but I felt I had to protect you from my sadness. (breathes and cries) I feel like I've spent so much in my life protecting other people's lives.

In this current section, Coleen is able to express forgiveness by cancelling out her expectations that she had toward her mother growing up.

Therapist: Do you want to carry this resentment around towards your mom?

Coleen: No.

Therapist: Okay. Can you release your mother? Can you see if you can forgive her, maybe for the things that you really wanted from her, but for lots of reasons in her background and with your father it just wasn't there?

Coleen: Mom, I know you have tried. You really couldn't cope with my sadness, that it was too hard on you because you love me.

Mom: I really haven't been a very good coper.

Coleen: Well, I understand that now. I understand that and I really liked that you talked about my grandmother because I've wondered why I didn't feel connected to my grandmother.

Therapist: Coleen, can you release your mom from some of this?

Coleen: Sure, I . . . it's real hard for me to even face her. I know that you did courageous things, the best you possibly could.

Therapist: Can you make a statement about forgiveness?

Coleen: I totally forgive you.

Mom: I know you do, darling. I just know you do.

Coleen: It's just hard for me to face all of this. (crying) It's been my role to take care of you. How can I hurt you? It's real hard.

Mom: But still I've got to know.

Coleen: I have to heal myself. It is my job now.

In this next segment, the therapist challenges Coleen on her statement that it's only her job to heal herself now. In a family-based approach, all members are encouraged to change their behavior toward one another, which not only aids in the healing from past wounds, but facilitates grounding the relationship toward future rebalancing of giving and taking from each other.

Therapist: No. Just wait a second. What do you need from Mom? Just tell her that. Tell her what you need from her when you're sad; it's not too late!

Coleen: I feel now that you can hear me when I'm sad.

Therapist: Tell her what you want for the future then.

Coleen: In the future, I want you to listen to my feelings.

Therapist: What do you think about that, Florence? Can you do that?

Mom: Absolutely. Coleen, I really want you to know I'm so grateful for this. I can see the way I'm like my mother. When it comes right down to it, I need to bring myself to say the things that need to be said.

Therapist: (To mother) What do you want your children to know?

Mom: How glad I am that we could be here together today.

Therapist: What do you want to express to Coleen?

Mom: I just know that she knows how much I have loved her all my life and how proud I am of her.

CLOSING FAMILY MEDITATION

In this last section, the therapist closes the session with a family meditation as a therapeutic ritual and he amplifies all the work that people did in the session and how further healing can take place. Some brief statements are made to one another about their future relationships.

Therapist: Why don't we just get back here and let's close our eyes and just take some deep breaths. I just want you to acknowledge how much we have accomplished today. Just maybe take a minute or so to acknowledge yourselves as well as each other for making this day happen. Special thanks goes toward Dad. And to acknowledge that there has been a lot of suffering as well as good times in this family, and that people did the best they could. And even though there's been misunderstandings and hurts in the past, perhaps you can remember all the positive things that you've said to one another and, at least, the future has the possibility of being different. There's negative actions that you may have done toward each other. See if you can just allow yourself to forgive yourself for anything you might have done. And remember that this is a special reunion, special relationships, special bonds. See if you can feel that connection. (silence) And in so keeping, open your eyes and look at each other. See if you can just make a simple statement about what you're feeling right now.

Ron: I'll try not to hurt any of you. If, at sometimes I do, it will be out of my frustration from our past relationships. I'll make efforts to drop the past. I'm sorry if I created any pain for any of you.

Coleen: You're forgiven. Mom, I realized I want to take care of you and also be who I am. I just don't want to take care of you and cut myself off from myself.

Mom: I don't ever want you to do that, dear.

Coleen: I want to take responsibility for myself first and be honest in how I care for you.

Mom: I know, dear. I don't have any uneasiness or discomfort about the way any of you are.

(Everybody spontaneously hugs as the session ends!)

Chapter 14

The Use of Self in Therapy

Gentle interventions, if they are clear, overcome rigid resistances. If gentleness fails, try yielding or stepping back altogether. When the leader yields, resistances relax.

Generally speaking, the leader's consciousness sheds more light on what is happening than any number of interventions or explanations.

Few leaders realize how much how little will do.

—From *The Tao of Leadership* by John Heider

Roberto Assagioli stated there are three ingredients in healing work: the technique, the timing of the intervention, and the consciousness of the healer. Many books have been written on the use of techniques, however, it is more difficult to convey how a therapist's state of consciousness can affect the therapeutic relationship. Can the healer's state of mind and how he consciously utilizes himself in the therapeutic encounter have impact on the outcome of the therapeutic endeavor? This chapter focuses on that question.

Satir (Baldwin and Satir, 1987) states:

I have learned that when I am fully *present* with the patient of the family, I can move therapeutically with much greater ease. I can simultaneously reach the depths to which I need to go and, at the same time, honor the fragility, the power, and the sacredness of life in the other. When I am in touch with myself, my feelings, my thoughts, with what I see and hear, I am growing toward becoming a more integrated self. I am more congruent, I am more "whole," and I am able to make greater contact with the other person. (p. 23)

Satir, in the opening line of the above quote, discusses the quality of being *present* with the patient or family in which you are working. Presence involves the fine balance of consciousness and will. Consciousness includes qualities of love, heart, Yin (Chinese word for a more receptive energy state), and being supportive. Will includes qualities of power, reflection, Yang (Chinese word for activity), becoming, director, and mind.

Embracing the above qualities involves utilizing one's whole personhood. Satir (Baldwin and Satir, 1987) states that we have an inner resource wheel that includes our body, emotions, mind, and our senses. In order to be fully present in the healing endeavor we need to activate and open each of these resources.

BODY

The healer needs to be in contact with his body. His body is his main tool to make contact with himself and the outside world. Being in contact with the body involves consciously paying attention to the sensations arising in it. Increasing attention to the body is the key to increased concentration, attention, and alertness. Concentrated focused attention is the most powerful element of making total contact with another human being.

Sharpening our attention and presence can be enhanced when we talk. Focusing on the quality of the texture of our speech can help a person to be very one-pointed in one's attention. Our voice can act as an anchor point and thus we can calm ourselves; this relaxed energetic state can permeate the therapeutic field and help to decrease reactivity in the person who is in therapy.

Being aware of gestures is also very important. The more positive your gestures (i.e., relaxed, smiling face), the more the client can tap into positive energy and hopefulness toward the future.

One of the most important resources in our body, both in ourselves and our clients, is our breath. The breath when fully open has the ability to allow ourselves to be in touch with what's emerging in the here and now that needs to be attended to and healed. It is also a direct channel where we can experience the depths and heights of our emotions.

FEELINGS

Being present means to allow ourselves to fully encounter our emotions. Our feelings can act as sensors to what is going on inside our client.

In a healing interchange, a client is sometimes working on allowing a part of oneself that has been disowned to express itself. Many times after exploring the client's will, he or she expresses the need to manifest a superconscious quality such as compassion, love, or forgiveness. The therapist can aid this process by meditating and consciously manifesting the quality that is flowering in the client. As the client is able to feel the sublime aspects of himself/herself and is able to feel his/her therapist resonate with this quality, a powerful bond takes place that is quite exhilarating and healing for both people. It is absolutely imperative for the therapist to experience the most vulnerable emotions including fear, anger, and grief. As one experiences these emotions, the client is able to let go of them. If the client is grieving a past or recent loss, and I am tearful, I do not hold back my own tears. My genuine feelings help the client to become more real and we form a very human connection. I also allow myself to emotionally show the client that I care about him/her.

Connecting emotionally with one's client, in my opinion, is the essential glue that helps to heal the deep psychic wounds. The client feels you are really with him; in this kind of connection, a deep trust permeates the therapeutic field. Both client and therapist experience they are being held and embraced. In this kind of connection the deepest vulnerabilities will manifest quicker and deeper, ready to be encountered and healed.

MIND

In a healing relationship, the therapist must not be locked into any one theoretical position to explain what is manifesting. Instead, the mind is flexible to many levels of understanding and conceptualizing what is emerging in therapy. Constructs are only helpful if the thought process and subsequent intervention leads to further growth and movement that one can see visibly in the therapeutic encounter.

Paradoxically, presence in the therapeutic relationship rests on a mental attitude of nonattachment about what "ought" to occur and the desire for some kind of measurable success. The fulcrum point of detachment on one side and involvement on the other will produce the balanced quality of presence that is needed in healing work.

Another major component of utilizing one's mind is our belief system about change. As expressed in previous chapters, healing work involves the belief that there is a healing agent in both you and the client. The purpose in counseling is to allow that wisdom to manifest itself. Respecting that there is this intuitive inner wisdom in the universe leads one to have an attitude that the healing relationship is a sacred spiritual connection.

INTUITION, IMAGINATION, CREATIVITY, AND THE SACRED

Another most powerful resource a therapist has is intuition. Intuition is a nonlinear concept since it involves perceiving a whole pattern all at once. It allows us to see more available choices for our responses and interventions.

The key to entering our intuition is through the faculty of imagination. Healers allow mental images to permeate their consciousness, which means to be in touch with each moment and see this moment as new and full of possibilities. Spontaneous images can allow us to intuitively know how to guide the client. The analogy is that of a surfer who must sense and feel himself in space; as the waves move one way, he adjusts his body slightly to spontaneously accommodate. This subtle balancing act is a prerequisite to healing work and imagination is a way of entering this primitive sensory realm.

The outcome of both therapist and client opening up to the multitude of inner resources allows for creativity and self-expression. There is a wealth of possibilities to manifest by ourselves and in our relationships with others. The gateway to this creativity is flexibility through allowing ourselves to open to all of our inner functions. Flexibility means not to be attached to any one mode of perceiving the world. If we can enter into the realm of the personal "I" (the eye of the hurricane), the superconscious opens up spontaneously, which is the seat of all creativity.

It is a prerequisite as a healer to have one's own meditation practice to disidentify from those things we naturally attach ourselves to. Through entering into this receptive place in our psyches, we can see the aesthetics of each moment and we see each new client and session with fresh eyes.

Chapter 15

Epilogue

This book has tried to address the need to include the spiritual dimension with the integration of the individual with couples and family systems healing. Emphasis was placed, in Chapter 3, in utilizing the experiential, humanistic, and transpersonal models as a bridge toward a paradigmatic synthesis. The rest of the volume tries to give theoretical and practical ways of entering a therapeutic healing process.

As I reflect on the volume, the emphasis placed on the therapist's own belief system about the healing endeavor is crucial. A belief that there is a wisdom in the human being ready to be tapped is a necessary ingredient for this kind of work. In addition, the belief that the human being has a spiritual nature is also a prerequisite to engage in profound therapeutic work. Finally, the focus on the development of the use of the self as the major therapeutic task is most important in producing therapeutic healing. Therapists need to feel comfortable with a variety of resources within themselves to maximize flexibility, creativity, spontaneity, and integrative abilities.

Since the use of self is crucial to the healing endeavor, it is extremely important for the therapist's training to include meditation, practicing presence, learning how to spontaneously work with what is emerging in both the individual and the system. This points to the development of needs for training institutes to develop a curriculum for working within the aesthetic dimension. Hopefully, this volume has addressed how one can integrate practical techniques, integrating them with the use of self of the therapist.

In closing, I have included an excerpt from an interview I did with Virginia Satir that focuses on what she says in her last will and testament including a reflection on her personal life, as well as thoughts about the future of psychotherapeutic healing. This brief excerpt is followed by a meditation by Satir.

Sheldon: Virginia, is there any last thing you'd like to say to any budding family therapists or family therapy colleagues about yourself or anything about family therapy we haven't talked about?

Virginia: If I were to say this was my last will and testament, one of the things I would say is that people have been tremendously kind and responsive to me–very kind and responsive and real. I couldn't have done it on my own here unless there was energy in the world for that and today there's a lot of energy because we're learning that we're moving away from a pathological to a holistic view of human beings and there's a lot of people open to that–but in relation to the population of five billion human beings on the face of this earth, it's really a very small group, but there is more emerging. So I feel good about what my life has been. I'm still on the front of all kinds of things, but that's only because I like it–I love it! I want to meet all those five billion people in the world, but unfortunately I won't.

Sheldon: Is there anything else you want to say to those colleagues or people in general about family therapy and healing?

Virginia: I just think we are all doing the best we can do and together a lot of things happened. What I hope is that people will keep looking for what's there and integrating rather than put blinders. I'm a psychoanalyst; I'm a transactional analyst; I'm whatever–Satirian, that's even worse. But rather, let's use all that we have received as a resource to tease out what it means to be more fully human. We're at the beginning of something, not at the end.

SATIR CLOSING MEDITATION

Gently close your eyes. Allow yourself to breathe fully. Your breath will come in effortlessly but the nurturing that it can do in your body is up to you by how tense or relaxed your body is. And now, as you are in touch with your breathing, be aware that your breath brings in nurturing ingredients to your body. For a moment, in a gentle way, let yourself be in touch with the feeling of breathing and your body responding. And while this is going on simultaneously would you give yourself a message of appreciation for you.

It could sound something like, "I love me. I value me." Recognize as you're doing this that this is a way to help you be strong. It is not a comment on your being better than anyone else. It's a loving way to keep you in good shape. I love me. And if today any little things run through your mind that remind you of all the mistakes you made, just smile and let the idea go by. Noting it, but that's all. And now let yourself go deep inside to a place where you keep the treasure that is called by your name. And as you go to that sacred place, deep within, notice your resources–your ability to see, hear, touch, taste, and smell; to feel and to think; to move and to speak; and above all to choose; to choose out of all of that which you have at this moment–that which fits you well. And then notice that which you no longer need. Once it fit you well but now it is no longer useful. Could you smile at it, gently take it out of your psychological closet and, with a blessing, let it go? And notice now that you have space for new possibilities and that you have all that you need in order to create that which you need or want and yet do not have. Now, also, become aware that armed with these wonderful resources acknowledge yourself as a child of this universe, as a being in this universe, that you are connected to the energy from the center of the earth which is there always, moves up through your feet and legs, your thighs and torso, bringing with it the energy of groundedness, the ability to be rational, cognitive, and reasonable, which we need very much. Now be in touch with the energy of the heavens, as it moves down through our head, face, and neck; into our chest and torso, bringing with it the energy of inspiration, of imagination, of sensing, of intuition; that which brings color and texture to our lives. And as these two energies come together, like two wonderful trees in the forest, the vibrations between them create a third energy–a willingness to allow what is inside to move outside to those who are ready with their eyes, with their ears, or their actions, ready to meet us and give back an energy. And for those who are not yet ready, can we notice them, let ourselves give love messages and move on? We don't have to ask people to be where they are not. So, at this moment be aware that you as a being in this universe are always fully nurtured when you let yourself remember. It's not a matter of getting it, it's only a matter of connecting with what already is there . . . . Can you also, at this time, give yourself permission perhaps even more than you've ever given yourself before, to look at everything, to listen to everything, to inquire about things? But then to swallow only that which fits for you, so you are no longer under a tyranny of what you should be, but only creating and taking, partaking of the resources around that fit you at this moment in time . . .

. . . Now, to help you with that I want to give you a gift; the self-esteem maintenance kit. The first thing in this kit is a detective hat which you try on as any good detective will do; to look, to inquire, to notice before you judge. The next thing in this kit is a medallion that you can wear around your neck. On one side are beautifully jeweled letters and it says YES. Underneath YES it says THANK YOU FOR NOTICING ME. What you are asking me at this point in time fits beautifully so the answer is yes. On the other side in beautifully jeweled letters is the word NO. THANK YOU FOR NOTICING ME, it says underneath. What you ask of me at this time doesn't fit at all, so thank you. You wear this around your neck, and while you're still alive you can always flip your medallion to what you want to say, so that never again will you put yourself in the position of saying yes when you feel no, or no when you feel yes. The third part in your self-esteem maintenance kit is a courage wand which when you want to move in the direction of your desires, hold this comfortably in your hand because it empowers you to move to a place you have never been, and also is perfectly willing to move with you dragging your fear behind you. The next thing in your kit is your wisdom box; the wisdom box, which is located behind your navel, halfway between your navel and your heart. This is your connection to the order of the universe; to all the intelligence of the universe. It is also that part which is the still small voice, it's that place where our wisdom resides and every human being has it. It has been covered up by negative rules or shoulds, but you have this, your wisdom box. It holds all the wisdom that is in the universe. Now, the last thing in the box is a golden key that allows you to ask anything, look at anything, try anything–without regard for what you have done, what you've tried, seen, or heard. That will be up to what fits for you. And now, at this point, I lovingly place this kit within you to take with you to be useful for the rest of your life. And also remember again, you are a manifestation of life as I am and therefore subject to all the nurturing there is in the universe. We have but to claim it, work with it, to accept it. I would like now for you, if it so fits, in the state where you are, to remember anyone you know–political figures, personal friends, family member–who need energy for healing. And if you will, give yourself permission to send energy without any strings, with only the note I LOVE YOU. I want you to have it to use for your own in your own way. Count yourself in also if you feel you need it . . .

Appendix I

**Virginia Satir Interviewed by Sheldon Z. Kramer
on Her Personal and Professional Growth
and History of Family Therapy
January 23, 1988**

Sheldon: Okay, I'm here in San Diego with Virginia Satir and I'm talking about the early beginnings of family therapy and her contributions. Okay, Virginia, let's talk about your development and your career as a therapist. What comes to you around your beginning?

Virginia: Two things. When I was five I wanted to be a children's detective on parents. That means what I was observing–what was going on–didn't make any sense, and so my goal was to make sense out of it. And I remember thinking: I'm going to be a children's detective on parents. Now this was just prior to a very serious life-threatening illness that I had which came about six months afterwards and I saw a whole lot of things with my parents and how they handled the illness that didn't make sense. And today I'm talking about it with the benefit of some logic and understanding that I didn't have then, except that what I had then was a strong intuitive sense–there was something more that I needed to learn. That was one thing.

The other thing was that I was somebody who never wanted to settle for being an armchair expert. I was sick to death of people who talked about people without knowing. I was addicted to the facts about people, so I gave myself permission–in fact, a requirement–that I spoke from experience. And when experience did not match the theories, I turned off the theory. That was something inside of me that's followed me all the time. Most people think theory first and make the experience match the theory and they throw out their experience. But that was something that followed me all the time because I watched the experience first and I've found that people criticize me for it, since people take the theory first. And I wasn't like that.

Sheldon: Even as a small child you weren't like that.

Virginia: Absolutely.

Sheldon: Could you talk a little about your early family background, parents and–

Virginia: Well, my families–both sets of grandparents–were farm families. Both my grandfathers came from Germany. They were very healthy, determined people willing to work hard and do, with a German background and a strong moral sense, and all that you know you must work hard. They came to this country. I was born in the house my grandfather, uh, built for his family. I was born in the same house my father lived.

Sheldon: Where was that?

Virginia: In Wisconsin, in the rural area of Wisconsin. So I knew hard work which, for me, was not a terrible burden. I always worked hard and working hard never seemed to be a burden to me. It was a part of my use of myself in life.

Sheldon: So were you kind of programmed early to use yourself?

Virginia: Oh yes, oh yes. And creatively, always creatively.

Sheldon: From childhood it was instilled in you?

Virginia: Oh yes. I remember our Christmas tree . . . remember I was born in 1916 and by the time I remembered a Christmas tree I was probably three years old . . . and so we didn't have Christmas tree ornaments. I suppose they were around, but we didn't have them on the farm, so we made them. Paper, we took little things, dried things, and we strung popcorn and our tree was always lovely, but it was always a creation of us and I still to this day pride myself on my own creativity. There was a time when you used to come to my house for dinner, you didn't have any prepared food because I made all my breads and jams and jellies and everything from scratch and still to this day. I am against using prepared foods. But sometimes we have to. But I felt the world was a place where I was really in it and doing and I give to the world. The world owed me nothing. I still believe that. I give to the world; the world doesn't have to give to me.

Sheldon: Were you close with both of your parents?

Virginia: I was in a way. I was very clearly the person in my family that both my parents took pride in, but they were not a family that showed affection. I remember times were poor in the Depression and my father gave me his last $5.00 for my books and he said, "Now it's my last $5.00, but it is important for you to have it." I knew really clearly that my parents loved me very much and also they loved the other kids. But I knew I had a really special place. I was the firstborn, the oldest one, and I was supposed to be the only one, but then twins followed me, and then my sister and brother. I had open opportunity to keep learning. Never had anybody tell me that I had to limit myself. But neither did I have false things–dreams. I had dreams, but I could live my dreams.

Sheldon: What I'm picking up is the emotional closeness wasn't there.

Virginia: Well, there are different types of emotional closeness. I never worried about whether my parents cared about me or not. We were on a very different track. My mother and father–neither one was educated in a formal sense–but they respected and they made possible for us all to get advanced education. And there was closeness, and you see, to me closeness means trust and we had that.

Sheldon: And you had twin siblings. Male? Female?

Virginia: Both male.

Sheldon: And what's the age difference between you?

Virginia: Just 18 months. See I grew up at 18 months when they were born. I became independent early. I learned to read at three.

Sheldon: Uh–what was your relationship with your siblings?

Virginia: With . . . well, you see, here I am . . . between two boys that were a unit between themselves and I was a unit out here. There were three units in my family–me alone, my twin brothers, and then my sister and brother. I was very close to my youngest brother and one of their friends and it still exists today.

Sheldon: And why don't you trace for me how it was you became interested in family therapy?

Virginia: Oh well, remember when I was born in 1916, Freud had not even published . . . remember that . . . so we can't talk about therapy because it wasn't there. But the way of dealing with troubled people was that they were banished and punished or exorcised . . . and criticized and such . . . Freud didn't write his book until 1918.

Education was the most important route there to everything for me and what was open to me was teaching or secretarial work or nursing. My mother didn't think nursing was a proper thing for me and that left education and secretarial work. I didn't like secretarial work . . . uh, so I became a teacher . . . a very creative teacher. And I also was very clear about whatever I was going to be it was going to be the very best that could happen. I never got into a competition with anybody . . . I got my degree in 1935. In those days, it was very deep in the middle of the Depression. It felt to me like the Depression would continue the rest of my life. Therefore, I was credentialed in special education, primary education, secondary education, and elementary education and I could teach art, and commercial subjects, and history. I got all that credentialing.

Sheldon: What year was this?

Virginia: 1936 . . . one year after social security came in, one year after this country almost became bankrupt or could have become communist at that time. So I decided. I was the third one in class to be placed and it was natural for me the first day of school to say to the children, well, "who would like to take me home with you?" I taught six years and I went home with a kid every day from Monday to Friday and I began to see all kinds of things that were upsetting. I had a network of very supportive parents so my discipline problems were very low . . . and any discipline problem I had no trouble settling. But one time, just as an illustration, I had a kid one day who was sleeping on his desk and the thing I said was, "Paul, what happened?" and he said, "My father got drunk last night and locked me out and I had to spend the night outside." So I had to look into that and I talked to his father. And remember I was at the ripe old age of twenty and I said, "I heard that Paul was out last night because you were drunk and locked him out." And I told him that it just can't happen because Paul needs his sleep and I said to him, "You have to stop drinking"—and he did. Then I began to see all kinds of other things and I realized that there were some ways that people were behaving that I didn't understand. Always in the back of my mind was how you make sense out of this because there was very little in those days to tell you about anything. Social work, per se, while we had a lot of doing good for people, it was just beginning to reach some dimension of being professional. But it had caring . . . there were schools and such like, but they were mostly around social welfare.

Sheldon: So it sounds like your work with families evolved right out of your teaching methods?

Virginia: Well, only in one manner of speaking. I was familiar with the families . . . but now when I started to go to graduate school I had to leave all that because the base of my first work was Freudian psychoanalytic training in psychotherapy. Freud considered the family members as enemies. Understanding people's behavior in the Freudian sense, it was from a pathological model. There was nothing healthy about it. So I had to leave the whole idea of family if I wanted to get my degree.

Sheldon: When did you start in social work?

Virginia: About age twenty-two.

Sheldon: You didn't spend too much time as a teacher?

Virginia: I spent six years as a teacher; I went to social work school in summer.

Sheldon: Oh, you went to school while you were teaching?

Virginia: Yes, there was no other way.

Sheldon: Where did you go to social work school?

Virginia: At Northwestern University for the first summer and they went out of business, and then to the University of Chicago.

Sheldon: How long did it take you to complete your social work training?

Virginia: Well, remember, war broke out December 7, 1941 and this is 1937, 38, 39 . . . and summer school . . . and then I got married and then I go full-time for a semester at the University of Chicago and my husband went overseas and I completed my training.

Sheldon: What year was that?

Virginia: 1942.

Sheldon: Now what started happening inside of you after the teaching and you've gone through a few years of social work school part-time, what started to shift your thinking from the pathological model at that time to more of the growth model?

Virginia: Well, when you're in school, it's easy for you to buy all the rhetoric . . . when I went to Florida, which was the last place my husband and I were before he went overseas . . . I was in an agency there and when you're practicing you ask yourself, "What have I learned?" And what I had learned didn't have much to do with helping these people. You see, I have always been someone who says, "All right, if that doesn't work, I'll try something else" and so I worked with foster home families, preparing foster home families, foster kids . . . and I knew for myself that I had to get everyone involved . . . in relation to that, but I didn't know I wasn't supposed to do that . . .

Sheldon: That just sort of came out of your experience?

Virginia: Well, it was sensible, wasn't it? . . . practical and human, like for instance, it never occurred to me to ask whether they went to church or not, but for a lot of people it was an important requirement for foster home families whether you went to church or not . . . well, whatever. To me, it didn't make much difference . . . to me, I wanted to see were they warm, were they accepting, were they able to connect? . . .

Sheldon: Do you think that your training in social work helped your own growth process in working with families?

Virginia: It had nothing to do with it. We were learning to be junior psychiatrists . . . it had nothing whatsoever to do with families.

Sheldon: You were being trained to be an individual therapist?

Virginia: That's right, absolutely.

Sheldon: So what is it that started this transition for you?

Virginia: What I learned didn't help me particularly. I was working with the kids from the court and all the stuff I learned didn't work. I was working with a woman who had never had a bit of training . . . she studied philosophy and she was a brilliant woman and she was head of the organization. She just came and we teamed up and we were a wonderful pair.

Sheldon: What was her name?

Virginia: Ruth Topping, just a wonderful, wonderful woman . . . so we were there helping the kids make their lives better.

Sheldon: How did you know that?

Virginia: From my intuition. You see, my cognition follows my intuition.

Sheldon: So foster care work was one transition in working with families?

Virginia: And that was all voluntary . . . then they offered me a job after I had volunteered there for about six months.

Sheldon: What did you learn there? What did you observe about these families?

Virginia: Well, I observed that they were all doing the best they could and they were available and I enjoyed them. I think it's important to enjoy the people I work with. You were supposed to be "professional" and that meant that you didn't have any fun and you didn't touch and you were supposed to be totally objective . . . it's an awful way to live your life. I couldn't stand that.

Sheldon: So you found yourself connecting with your own person-hood . . . what else influenced you other than the foster care?

Virginia: Remember there was no such thing as family therapy then . . . forget that. It's not there. What we're doing is working to help people . . . alright . . . so I got a reputation for dealing with difficult people. I supervised and specialized and I said to myself, "Why can't the others be successful with these difficult cases? What was so different about me?" Well, I listened to other professionals talk and I said, "That talk doesn't interest me . . ." and that was talking in what I call dirty language.

Sheldon: What do you mean by that?

Virginia: No. You see, Sheldon, before I die, there's one idea I want to get across. When you meet somebody, you don't say to yourself, "How should I do this?" and then go back to some book or something and figure out what you ought to be doing. People are doing that all the time and making terrible mistakes. What you do is, you see what's here and then you say, "Okay, what do I have to begin to shed light on this? If I don't have it, then I create it."

Sheldon: So that's what happened to you.

Virginia: Sure.

Sheldon: And so it came natural for you in the context you were dealing with at that time?

Virginia: And I never could buy the idea that people were essentially bad. There were some terrible things, but nothing was really bad. I already knew that this was what people learned. I also knew how available people could be. Psychological terminology was not useful. Freud was one of my mentors, but not because of psychoanalysis, but because he was willing to stick his neck out and to set the world with new ideas where we could see that we had an inner self that could direct us negative or positive; that was a new thing.

Anyway, so I was always a maverick . . . you see, what was interesting is I took the people that nobody else wanted. So I didn't get any criticism; they were always relieved. And then I couldn't stand the restrictions of an agency because I wasn't speaking the same language . . . and you know, I can't imagine, I don't know if you've ever seen those early assessment sheets–they were awful.

Sheldon: Why don't you give an example of your professional life . . . back in that time . . . when you were sitting in a conference meeting. What would go through your mind?

Virginia: Well, they wouldn't have known what I was talking about and when I saw at one point the people flipping a coin for a diagnosis, I said, "There's something wrong with this." And it was something that hit me how people spoke: pontificated and categorized. I knew that these people who I worked with did the best they knew.

Sheldon: You never liked to categorize people. Is that right?

Virginia: I wasn't interested in becoming a labeler and I worked, as I say, with lots of people. I also learned to keep my mouth shut and I also learned I didn't have to listen to these other professionals.

Sheldon: So what I'm getting from you is that you discovered the most important thing early on in your career . . . how you connected with others and saw your educated colleagues disconnected from people–either with words or labels they used to distance themselves more–is that accurate?

Virginia: I couldn't stay in a context where people were devaluing people and I also knew . . . the medical movement was the wrong way of looking at things . . . so anyway, I went into private practice of social work. I was the second social worker in Chicago to go into private practice and everybody said, "You're crazy" but I needed a context and at that time, it was only that I wanted to treat people differently. I made use, positive use, of stuff I had learned, but I asked myself first, "How does somebody get depressed? Why is there no energy?" Well, "Why are they doing that?" And to see that they're using it for something else instead of where they're living and using it to pull themselves together . . . so that is oversimplifying . . . so I worked with people that nobody else would . . . and I had . . . and I also believed that I needed a sliding scale so my fees were from $1.00 to $7.50. This was 1951.

Sheldon: So you just started to just work on your own. Private practice?

Virginia: Yes. And I was willing to take the risk . . . I had no other way of making an income, but what I say to people when I did that . . . I had to make my living at it . . . so I couldn't have any catastrophes . . . I couldn't get insurance . . . I was working with the highest risk people that there were, and in order to be alive, I had to be good.

Sheldon: So what kind of people did you work with?

Virginia: Mostly schizophrenics and people who were listed as mentally retarded . . . who were involved in the court . . . these kinds of people.

Sheldon: So you were working solo?

Virginia: Totally. Totally alone.

Sheldon: Did you have any colleagues you could share with?

Virginia: No, there was no such thing. There was nobody who knew anything. What I would do would be . . . people knew that I was being helpful and they sent me all kinds of people and I helped them and I said, "Would you like to know what I'm doing?" And they would listen but they didn't understand and, at that time, I didn't show how to help them . . . . I didn't show people, but when I came to California I showed people. Well, I did demonstrations after a while because talking wasn't adequate. So the people that I came in contact with first were some physicians. See, I was accepted by the medical profession before I ever was by anyone else because I had doctors who really were with me, who helped me. They didn't know what I was doing, but they knew it was good. I was also working with psychosomatic difficulties because I was interested in how the body manifests what's going on inside and that was also what helped me to know about sculpting.

Sheldon: What do you really think made you feel effective with people?

Virginia: I could love people.

Sheldon: You started feeling love for the people?

Virginia: I felt it always . . . but in the beginning, it wasn't okay for me to let myself show it.

Sheldon: In other words, you removed the block from being able to give that sense of caring to others?

Virginia: Yes, I decided I didn't have to be professional. Another day I remember is in 1956. I'm in my office and I see an article called, "Toward a Theory of Schizophrenia" by Don Jackson and his colleagues and they were describing what I was seeing and I said, "Hallelujah! Somebody else knows." That's why I took the job two years later and I called him and that's how come we got connected. But there was also something else–I read a little blurb in 1955–Carmen Yarfus in Chicago. I never knew how he knew about me, but he asked me to come and teach what I knew about family dynamics–this was after I had seen over 400 people . . .

Sheldon: Who was Carmen Yarfus?

Virginia: Carmen Yarfus was the superintendent of the Chicago State Hospital. He was also newly appointed director of the Illinois State Psychiatric Institute . . . . Illinois was 39th or 40th in the new list of care for the psychiatric hospital in 1951. Rudy Novak and Jerry Horvath–both community psychiatrists–activated a group of people so that we could support a bill to get some of the money earmarked for psychiatric patients to be put in good programs that would be involved in psychiatric training–this was a pilot program and Carmen asked me to be on the faculty . . . I was the only woman on the faculty and everybody had to go through my training. That was 1955; I left in 1958.

Sheldon: Did you follow other therapists who were doing similar things like you were?

Virginia: Yes, I saw a clip somewhere about Murray Bowen, who was hospitalizing schizophrenics. You see, in those days, Dr. Rosen was the only one doing anything with schizophrenics–quote/unquote. He was regarded as "way out." People were not that interested in what he was doing. They thought he was crazy anyway. When I saw what Murray was doing, I called him and asked to come and see him because I thought something might be happening that was similar and that was also in '56; he was very courteous and wonderful to me. He showed me everything that he was doing with his families and I told him what I was doing . . . I also became familiar with Nathan Ackerman.

Sheldon: This is 1956?

Virginia: Yes, 1956. Nathan Ackerman had published a paper in 1934 about the patient in relation to the family, but it didn't go anywhere because that was the heyday of psychoanalysis . . . . I hadn't met Nathan at this point, but Murray was the first one that I knew. I also met Don Jackson and his colleagues who were working out in California and the Peachtree Group with Carl Whittaker and his colleagues in Atlanta and we were all looked upon as kind of peculiar–but these were exciting times. There was Lyman Wynne and Alice Corneiliason and Ted Leitz at NIMH and they were all discovering similar things about families.

Sheldon: Who was the first person you contacted in family therapy?

Virginia: Murray and I became good friends. He came out to California and at that time he was in a precarious way because he was doing something very much outside of psychiatry and he didn't know what might be . . . you know, he had started a very successful training program at Georgetown, so at that time everybody was by themselves.

Sheldon: Did Murray influence you at all?

Virginia: Murray didn't know anything I didn't know. In fact, I had a lot of experience with families–by 1958 I'd seen more than 400 families.

Sheldon: Did you collaborate with him at all?

Virginia: No, he was there and I was here . . . what I did was translate what he was doing for some of the residents. You see, nobody collaborated with anybody because, you see, we knew we were outside the pale.

Sheldon: So when you contacted these people, it was just curiosity . . . in seeing what other people were doing because probably you were seeing something similar to what you've been doing–working in a vacuum and suddenly you see others doing something similar that caught your interest and curiosity?

Virginia: That's it exactly . . . and there were no connections between people that I knew about . . . maybe there were some that I didn't know about. This was in 1956.

Sheldon: What was the next step in your development?

Virginia: I called up Don Jackson on the nineteenth of February, 1959, and I told him who I was . . . told him that I'd read his articles and he said, "Come see us." At that time he was working with Gregory Bateson, Jay Haley, John Weakland, Gil Frye, and himself. So I presented halfway through and Don said, "I want you to come and help. There is a young resident that's just finishing his residency named Jules Riskin. He plans to come and there's a place for you to start." So I said, "okay" and I came down and that's where that started.

So, on March 19, 1959, exactly one month after I called him, we opened the doors of the institute which was an old broken-down house, where you walk on a step and you fell through. I did a live family demonstration there every Wednesday and taped it. People came to watch me do that and we were developing a research project, but I didn't like research so I said, "I don't want that, I'll take training." We started training in September of 1959; I became head of the training. The Mental Research Institute started out with the idea of looking at the relationship between interaction in family members as it related to helping those families.

Sheldon: What was your main role in the continuing of the development of MRI?

Virginia: I was a trainer . . . it was very separate . . . very separate. I did the training–I always had grants then–there was the other part where they did their theoretical business.

Sheldon: Did you collaborate at all?

Virginia: No, there was no collaboration.

Sheldon: So you were still working–even though you were in a group–you were still working in isolation?

Virginia: Because there was no collaboration possible . . .

Sheldon: It was like the left brain talking to the right brain.

Virginia: Right, exactly right. And that was one of the reasons I left . . . there was no way that I . . . no way that these people could hear me. And I got tired of this male charade.

Sheldon: Do you want to elaborate on that?

Virginia: Well, these guys get together and talk and it seems to me that they were seeing who could outdo whom.

Sheldon: So you saw the competitiveness there and–

Virginia: Oh gosh, yes!

Sheldon: And then that negativity took you away from there?

Virginia: Yes.

Sheldon: Okay, so where did you go then . . . after you left MRI?

Virginia: Well, Esalen . . . I'd found Esalen by 1964 and I learned about this place that was directly from Gregory Bateson. Gregory was one of the people I loved, respected, and valued very much.

Sheldon: What did Gregory tell you?

Virginia: He said there were two people I needed to meet–one was Alan Watts and the other was Don Kiyakowa. And Gregory and I were extremely good friends. I respected Gregory and I believed him. Now Don Kiyakowa was a semanticist and Alan Watts was a Buddhist–and I didn't know about either one. So, then, because I believed Gregory, I saw in the paper a notice that Alan Watts was going to have an evening lecture about his book, so I went there. And this was my entrance into the people who were considered the counterculture, and I listened. I'd never heard any of this stuff before. It sounded like what I had known a long time ago.

Sheldon: It was connected to you.

Virginia: VERY connected to me . . . and at this lecture there was a flyer for Esalen. I followed up with going to Esalen. That night, I went to Esalen. I reached Esalen–I'm all dressed up, I'll never forget–black velour hat, an orange leather suit, leopard shoes, make-up. And I went to Esalen and here were people . . . with earrings, breasts hanging out, no shoes, barefoot, women nursing all over the place and I said, "My goodness, what did I get into?"–at first, for a straight one like me–

Sheldon: A farm girl?

Virginia: A farm girl, but then I kept thinking: Gregory said I needed this and it would be good for me. And I trusted him so I went in. I was in a world I'd never seen before . . . I'll never forget any of them . . . and so I went in the door and a man came toward me and said, "Are you Virginia Satir?" and I said, "Yes." He said, "Will you go to the baths with me tonight?" and I think to myself, "Well, I really am in a den of iniquity." But I have to act as though I'm cool, so I'm cool . . . but I didn't know anything.

Sheldon: How old were you then?

Virginia: Well, that was 1964. So I was 46 years old.

Sheldon: And this was all new to you?

Virginia: Absolutely new. I knew from nothing. I was brought up a nice girl–anyway–So I heard about all these orgies . . . and so this was 5:30 and this date was going to be at 11:30, six hours, and I ruminate, rehearse–I'm in this funny place–beards–and whatever I see here, but I am cool about things like that on the outside. I kind of sit back and observe, but where I was with that was rehearsing, would I or wouldn't I? And then when he came for me he had five other men with him and I thought, "Oh, my worst fears"–'cause I'd read about these awful places. So we go down to the baths like that, you go out of the lodge and down to the baths. I'm whistling, I'm trying to keep calm . . . well, I want to tell you, I turned a corner into the baths and all that stuff left me because it was a beautiful place on the ocean and the tubs were filled with people . . . they were singing and guitars were playing and . . . I took off my clothes and that was the end of all that stuff.

Sheldon: A new transformation.

Virginia: Absolutely . . . and then I brought my trainees up there within two months. I find out there was another life which is called the affective life that I didn't know anything about and here I met people that were talking about the things I could connect with. All this started in 1963.

Sheldon: It was really the heart of the counterculture revolution.

Virginia: Right . . . sure and I became one of the directors in 1964. They asked me if I would be a director. At that time, they were doing weekend seminars and I said, "I'd like to bring my group down here for a week." So I initiated week-long seminars and later I initiated month-long seminars. So I was beginning to bring my group down here for all the wonderful things offered that stimulated the right brain–intuition and creativity. And there's music and dance. And altered states of consciousness. This is where I learned about biofeedback from Alice and Elmer Green. Here is where I began to meet the people in the world I began to respect. I understood more about the body. This was the middle of the 60s and the emphasis was on unleashing emotion. However, I told myself that, "Just because you're into your right brain, don't lose your left one." So I was for thought and feeling . . . and I got some flack for that.

Sheldon: There wasn't a balance there–it was more one extreme.

Virginia: That's right. So after 1969, I couldn't stand it there anymore. Because Esalen was off-balance in the direction of feeling. I felt that I came to another place where there was another should–"You should always be open" and that's the same as "You should always be closed"–so it was 1969 when I left. I went totally into my own private practice which began to be both an office practice (which I had all along anyway) and then it just flowered into more and more training–more and more seminars, and so on and so forth.

Sheldon: So again, you went back to yourself?

Virginia: That's right. That's right. It's always been that way.

Sheldon: Your original work seemed to be mostly with families, certainly *Peoplemaking* and *Conjoint Family Therapy* and then over the last years it has seemed to extend beyond working with families. I heard you say at one time that you no longer limit yourself by calling yourself a family therapist–could you talk more about this transition in your work?

Virginia: Once you get a picture, a family is a group, all the things that go on in a family go on in any group. So it was easy for me to make the transition from family, where things are learned to any other group–to an institutional or work group and to see that the same things were present. So then I saw that the family was the incubator for people, but since they took what they learned into the outside world, the world became a reflection of that incubator. I began to work in groups doing families when I began reconstructions which I began at least twenty-five years ago. Whatever context I find myself. I work with process–individual, family, or groups.

Sheldon: Now, one thing you said before–if I hear you clearly, Gregory Bateson was a kind of pivot point that told you to go see Alan Watts and through that these next transitions took place. Do you think Bateson influenced you?

Virginia: Gregory was a totally unblaming person. He knew observation better than I did. Good anthropology is good observation. You see, one thing I didn't tell you before–I was deaf for two years and during that time I was sick and that's where I learned to really concentrate and really see–so by some miracle I got hearing in one ear and later on I got it in both ears. Gregory was a superior observer; he also was a superior connector in his own right. If you read Gregory–some of it is quite obtuse, you have to really read it–but Gregory was able to put things together and it was there to be looked at. He was an extremely bright man. He was interested in the human condition. He was the best I know of as an observer and his conclusions were his observations–NOT his opinions. And I have that part of me that is very careful and clear about how I use my observations.

Sheldon: Today, many people call you a healer. Could you talk just a little bit about that and how that fits in with your earlier background?

Virginia: Well, you have to remember that what I say may have no truth in it at all. But see, I don't see how any therapist can not be a healer. If you take what is happening right now and change it, that has to do with healing. You're healing something. You see, before people talked about healing. They'd say somebody gets well, maybe or maybe not even that–there was a change of behavior. We've been afraid to talk about the absolutely fantastic thing we want to do which is to heal the pain in the person. Now, if you think that people do bad behavior because it's a whim, that is not so . . . destructive behavior is costly and pain-producing for everybody, including the person who does it.

Dysfunctional behavior comes from wounds inside–we don't have these wounds when we're born; these wounds are created and so you could say that the symptomatology is that which shows us that we have wounds. Healing is a word associated with religion. And when therapy was looked upon as something objective and, heaven only knows what else–professional–there was no room for healing. But that's what good therapy resulted in. The wounds were somehow healed and the person was able to take on things for themselves–to handle their own life . . . so it's very clear to me and to the people around me . . . I never did follow the idea that I was going to take a technique and push it–my total idea was "How can the wounds be healed? How can the person come to be in charge of themselves? How can they have a relationship with other people that works?"

Sheldon: What do you think about being the earliest woman pioneer in the field of family therapy?

Virginia: There was no other woman there. For years and years and years.

Sheldon: What are your thoughts about that?

Virginia: Let me put it this way. Don Jackson and I were the first . . . because we were connected with the Institute and Don and I were the first ones. I had a connection with Murray Bowen and others. These were all men. All right–they didn't have connections with each other. This is all a group of loners. That we would have conferences where we could come together and I was the only one who was willing to deal with these men. I never cowtowed to them; I respected them in terms of who they were, etc. I also knew that none of them would feel they could take care of me. I also realized that they were fearful–they were all doctors, every one, and they had all paid a higher price for going out of the fold than I did . . . see I was free to do that, I was a woman and a social worker, and I wasn't beholden to anybody. Well, all these persons had a relation-ship with me–of one kind or another–and so that wasn't true of all the others.

Sheldon: Do you feel like you influenced many other people in family therapy?

Virginia: Well, read the American Family Therapy Association (AFTA) report in 1978. The AFTA report is a request for who influenced you the most–my name is way up top.

Sheldon: One last thing, Virginia. How would you like future family therapists to kind of view your work? What would you hope would happen in the family therapy field into the future?

Virginia: Well, one of the hopes I have is that people will learn how to love themselves–that's the first thing and yet, we're a long way from that. And that we would learn how to grow and that we could all be teachers–I'd like to get rid of the label therapists–instead, we could all be seen as teachers of how to become more fully human and we would look at the learning model as the paradigm of change–that we could expand our abilities to see the many ways in which human beings adapt instead of comparing.

Appendix II

Self-Help Guide to Mind-Body Relationship Tools:
Steps to Achieve Sacred Connectedness

The following section gives you step-by-step instructions for conducting the exercises that are discussed throughout this book. In addition, there are other tools here to help you begin or continue your individual and relationship journeys. These exercises and tools are the heart and soul of my program. As such, this section is an excellent guide for therapists who wish to do this work with their clients, or for individuals who wish to do their own work in this area, with or without the assistance of a professional counselor.

Many people in the helping professions have found that not only does this material give them detailed instructions for implementing this program in their own practice, but provides clients with "take home" material that can speed up the healing process tremendously.

As you read these exercises, you will note that I sometimes ask you to let an image of a person, place, or experience emerge in your mind. Some people report getting clear mental images when asked to do this; others do not get images but rather a *sense* of the object or person they are asked to imagine. This sense of the object, person, or past experience is not easy to describe since it does not appear to be based on sensations that we usually associate with our five senses. Instead, the process can be rather abstract. Whichever way you get these images is fine. The exercises seem to be equally effective whether you receive an actual mental image or instead have this more abstract *sense* of the object, person, or experience.

I am focusing here on tools to help couples, but individuals can also benefit from many of the exercises. You will find some suggestions for working directly with your family of origin.

I hope this volume and these exercises will aid you in understanding and activating what I call, "Optimal Relating." May you capture your own spirit inside and between you and others who mean the most to you!

SIX STEPS TO ACHIEVE SACRED CONNECTEDNESS

It would be helpful to record the following exercises on an audio-tape machine so that you and/or your partner can better focus on the processes. Through trial and error you will develop exactly the speed you need for reading these exercises so that you will feel relaxed and unrushed. The best way to do this is for one person to read as a second person follows the instructions. The reader should keep an eye on the person doing the exercise, adjusting the reading speed, faster or slower, as he sees the other person respond. While this requires some practice it is actually quite easy to do.

Step 1: Preparatory Meditations

Before you meditate, sit on a chair with your spine erect and your head upright and balanced. If you are working with a partner, place two chairs facing one another, with your kneecaps almost touching. Keep your hands in your lap or on your legs. Another way of doing this exercise is to sit on the floor with a soft cushion under your buttocks with your spine erect. If you are doing this with your partner have him or her also sit on a cushion facing you, and make sure that you are at eye level with one another.

> Focus on your breathing, in and out of your nose . . . allow the air of the in-breath and out-breath to flow gently through your nostrils . . . . Feel the subtle sensations beneath the nose as your breath moves in and out. Let your mind rest on this one point. If you find yourself being distracted, blow a little harder through your nose and once again focus on the inhale and exhale of your breath through your nostrils.

> Let your attention focus on the top of your head; feel the sensations on top of your head; experience them without judgment, maintaining the detached perspective of an observer. Now, gradu-

ally move your attention to your forehead and the back of your head, and once again just observe the sensations that are there . . . . Slowly move your attention to your cheeks . . . nose . . . and mouth . . . . Bring your attention to your neck and experience the sensations around your neck . . . . Bring your focus to your upper back and chest; experience the sensations in this area of your body . . . . Move your attention to your heart area and the middle of your back and your chest . . . slowly bring your attention to your stomach and lower back; experience the sensations emerging there . . . . Move your attention to your buttocks and genital area . . . . Bring your attention through the upper parts of your legs, slowly . . . . Keep focusing on your breathing while you do this exercise . . . . Move your attention down through your legs and eventually to your feet.

Slowly begin to bring your attention upward, from the bottom of your feet, up through your ankles, through your legs, genitals, pelvis, lower back and stomach, chest and back, upper back, and chest, through your neck, up through your mouth, nose, and cheeks, up through your forehead and back to the top of your head.

Sweep your attention up and down through your body as you focus on your breathing. As you continue to focus on your in-breath and out-breath (through your nostrils), and as you sweep your inner body, listen to the following words:

Breath nurtures the body. When you are tense and tight you are only partly nurtured, so the rest of you is hungry. The more tight you get, the more you feel others should feed you. Therefore, allow your body to be relaxed while breathing. You will soon develop an awareness of your trigger points, that is, areas of your body and your emotions where you react internally or project parts of yourself onto others.

This exercise can flow into Step 2, especially if you are doing it with your partner; however, if you are doing this alone you may want to go directly to Step 4F.

Step 2: Couples Meditation

Allow yourselves to gently close your eyes (or to continue to keep your eyes closed) and become aware of how you are sitting. If you need to change your position to relax yourself, do that now. Become aware of your breathing in and out of your nostrils. Focus your full attention on the air moving in and out of your nose. If you have any difficulty concentrating, breathe a little harder and quicker through your nose and come back to that one point where the air moves in and out of your nostrils. Take a deep breath through your nose, quickly, hold it, and let it go slowly through your mouth. Repeat this two more times. As you focus on your breathing, can you appreciate the life force moving in and out of you? Can you also acknowledge that the same life force is moving in and out of your partner? For a moment allow yourself, while focusing on your breathing, to acknowledge the special relationship you have with each other, the ups and downs you have experienced together, the commitment you have had in your life together up to this moment.

Silently acknowledge the special bond you have with one another. Allow yourself to keep focusing on your breathing, the air moving in and out of your nose as you slowly begin to open up your eyes and look at each other without talking. Keep being aware of your breathing. Just experience what is happening inside when you look at each other. (Do this for five to ten minutes.) When either one of you is ready to share what you are experiencing at this moment, as you look deeply into each other's eyes, allow yourself to talk now, sharing these thoughts with your partner.

After you finish sharing, go to Step 3.

Step 3: Communication

A. Focus on your breathing as you continue to slow yourself down. Check into your own thoughts and feelings and bodily sensations. Especially continue to focus on any feelings or body sensations emerging as you look silently at your partner. Just give yourself space to look and experience whatever is happening in the moment.

B. Take turns talking and listening. Always begin each communication with the word "I" (I think, I feel, I sense, etc.). Be sure that you do not blame one another for anything. Take responsibility for your own experience. It is best to describe to the other person what you are experiencing in your body. For example, you might say, "As we sit here, I feel a sort of fluttering in my stomach. I am feeling a little scared but also excited." Give each other a great deal of space to share this kind of intimate communication.

C. As you are communicating these things, put your hand on your body where you are experiencing the strongest sensations. Breathe into that place in your body. Describe the sensations you are feeling to your partner.

D. The person sharing needs to express what he or she is experiencing completely, with total honesty and truth. The listener just receives, even if it is painful to hear. If the listener starts to react internally and/or outwardly, it is important for that person to control his or her reactions and keep focusing on breathing and holding whatever he or she is experiencing. Tune into what your partner is saying to you even though you may not agree with it. This is the key to the power of reaching sacred connectedness.

E. As a listener, you then communicate back to your partner what you believe you heard your partner tell you. Do this in your own words. If you, as the listener, missed something or heard something incorrectly, your partner should repeat what he or she wants to communicate, and then the listener repeats back again. (Switch roles with the listener becoming the sharer and vice versa.) Make sure you communicate any conflicts that are occurring inside of you about yourself or the relationship.

Step 4: Inner Family Work

A. If either of you experiences strong pain or negative emotions when sharing with one another, especially shame, fear, anger, and/or grief, tell your partner that you need to go inside and do some inner work.

B. Both of you look at each other as you take some deep breaths and look each other in the eyes without talking.

C. The partner who heard the request for inner work needs to work on evoking an attitude of openness and caring. This can be achieved by focusing your attention on moments in your life when you experienced a sense of openness and caring. Show these qualities through your eyes!

D. If you are the person who requested to do inner work close your eyes and allow images, sensations, or thoughts to bubble to the surface, paying particular attention to your family of origin. Experience that pain and note where it manifests in your body.

E. If you are the partner working on manifesting qualities of openness and caring, continue to focus on your breathing and be a steady presence for your partner as he or she does this inner work. In addition, you will read the following exercise. Make sure that you read this exercise very slowly and give your partner time to process what is occurring inside.

F. Exercise:
Close your eyes (or continue to keep your eyes closed) . . . focus your attention (or continue to focus your attention) on the inhale and exhale of your breathing as you breathe through your nose. Allow images of your family of origin to appear spontaneously, including yourself in the house where you grew up and consider home. Are there any smells or colors inside your house that you can reexperience at this time? Look around. Note how the furniture is placed. Note where people are in the house. Note who is talking with whom. Who is closest to whom? Is anybody alone or

left out? What emotional atmosphere surrounds this family? How do people interact with each other? Is anyone in conflict with each other? How are they dealing with this conflict? Who is in the most pain? Go closer to the person who is in the most pain. It could be yourself. What does this person look like? What is the body posture? What does this person long for from others? If you experience any pain, allow that to be there and open yourself to experiencing it; see it as a gift to allow yourself to heal. Who is scared in this family? Go closer to those who are afraid, see what they look like and what they need. Who needs the most love in this family?

Allow your inner family members to talk with each other. Do this, completely verbalizing the conversations outwardly. Allow your inner family members, including yourself, to express their needs to each other. If there is any fear, anger, or grief, express it outwardly, even loudly, if you need to. Let the images speak from the heart.

Do the following alternative exercises if you know you need to work on very specific issues with your inner family–including your inner child connecting with your parents, or issues with your inner parents or with your inner siblings.

STRENGTHENING BOUNDARIES OF YOUR INNER CHILD

Do this exercise when you feel your inner child needs to be strengthened and healed in a relationship, such as being caught up in one's parental struggles.

Close your eyes and allow yourself to focus on each inhalation and exhalation of your breath through your nose. Let an image emerge of your inner child interacting with your parents. What are you experiencing with your parents? What is going on between the three of you? Are you getting too involved with

your parents' struggles? Do you need to see yourself as separate from them? If you do, allow yourself to begin to experience your own inner strength coming from your core, a
strength that is natural and which has been with you from the
time of your birth.

Allow yourself to stand up to your parents and tell them what
you need from them. Remember that you are in complete control right now. Have a clear sense of yourself as a child or
teenager, knowing yourself separate from your parents. Allow
yourself to feel your own power and not to merge with your
parents' images.

Begin to talk from this place of power and strength and tell
your parents what you need. For example, you might say, "I
know you have conflicts between you but these are not my
issues and I need you to acknowledge that to me." Continue to
experience your own sense of self, separate from your parents.

STRENGTHENING INNER PARENTAL MARITAL IMAGES

The following exercise should be done when you find yourself
repeating patterns in your own relationships that your parents had
with their marriage. This exercise is especially good if your parents
have never been able to resolve their conflicts.

Close your eyes and allow yourself to focus on your breath
moving in and out through your nose. Let an image of your
inner parents spontaneously emerge. What do they look like?
What expressions do they have on their faces? What are each
of them struggling with in their lives? What do they need from
each other?

Let them enter into a dialogue, with you acting as spokesper-
son, expressing their wants and needs out loud to each other.
Allow them to express the needs or wants they have toward
each other. Allow feelings that they have not expressed to

emerge. See if they can deal with their personal differences without feeling unloved and unappreciated. See if they can make different kinds of agreements so they both feel better. For example, one might say, "I don't like the way you discipline the children. I feel you are too strict." The other might say, "I hear what you are saying but I still believe that I must insist that they obey me." Let each of them take turns communicating.

STRENGTHENING YOUR INNER SIBLING IMAGES

This next exercise can be done if you have found yourself repeating old family patterns in your present relationship.

Close your eyes and focus on your breath moving in and out through your nose. Take a quick deep breath through your nose and slowly let it out through your mouth. Repeat three times. Come back to normal breathing through your nose. Let a spontaneous image form of you and your siblings in the house you then called home. Where are you? What do you and your siblings look like? How old are all of you? What are you doing? Are you together or apart? What feelings do you have toward one another? Do you look up to one of your siblings? Are you jealous of each other? Are you friends? Do you play with each other? How do you play? What do these siblings want from each other? What are they secretly needing from one another? Does anything need to change in their relationships? Let them talk aloud to each other about their relationships with one another. After you let each of them express their feelings, see if you can get them to negotiate their needs, perhaps working out compromises and resolving conflicts, so that they can relate in a more harmonious way.

HEALING THE INTRAGENERATIONAL FAMILY

Do the following exercise as a follow-up to the previous exercise on healing the inner family. This meditation works best when you know there needs to be healing with a parent because of extreme wounding that has taken place when you were a child. You can record this exercise on tape or have your partner or friend read it as you go inside and do this intricate inner work. It would be helpful to read Chapter 7 in this volume, which describes the kinds of experiences you might have as you heal your intragenerational family.

Contacting the Inner Child

Gently close your eyes. Begin to inhale and exhale through your nostrils. Do this very slowly. Allow yourself to fully concentrate on the point right under your nostrils as the air moves in and out of your nose. If you find yourself distracted, blow a little harder through your nostrils. Take a deep breath quickly through your nose, hold it for a moment and then let it out slowly through your mouth.

Allow an image of your inner child at any state of development to emerge spontaneously. Begin to see how he/she looks. What is he/she wearing? What kind of expression is on his/her face? What is his/her mood? Where is he/she? Continue to focus on your breathing and see this image outside of yourself. Let yourself fully take in everything you can about your inner child. Then see how he/she looks from a distance. It is important to keep your attention on your breathing when working with your inner family imagery.

When you have a clear image and sense of your inner child, take a deep breath quickly through your nose, hold it for a moment, and let it out slowly through your mouth. Repeat this two times. Bring the inner child into yourself fully, become him or her. Experience what it is like to be that child. How does your body feel? What are you experiencing emotionally? What are you thinking? Allow yourself to get in touch with your inner child's wounds. Experience his/her pain. Experience this in your body. Where in your body does it hurt now? Breathe into that point. Experience it fully!

Allow your inner child to express fully how he/she is feeling. Allow him/her to express his/her pain. Let your inner child express how he/she got to be the way he/she is. Let him/her express wants and needs. It is important to allow yourself to experience any strong sensations emerging in the body. It is also important to allow yourself to express outwardly what is going on emotionally. It is important to express fear, sadness, grief, and anger. Give your inner child permission to express itself fully. Allow yourself to express its pain.

After you have allowed your inner child to express itself fully and to have some degree of emotional release, take a deep breath quickly through your nose and hold it, letting it out slowly through your mouth. Repeat this two more times. Allow yourself to take the image of your inner child and put it outside yourself. See the inner child clearly in your mind as you give assurance that you will return later and will not neglect him or her. Put the inner child aside for a moment. Continue the next part of the exercise.

Accessing the Inner Parent(s) and Inner Child

Continue to focus on your breathing; inhale and exhale through your nose. Once again take a deep breath quickly through your nose, hold it, and then let it out slowly through your mouth. Repeat this at least two more times. Allow a spontaneous image to come of the parent with whom you need to do some healing work. See this image outside yourself as you continue to focus on your breathing. What does your parent look like? What is he/she wearing? What mood is your parent experiencing?

Allow yourself to take a deep breath quickly through your nose, hold it, and then let it out slowly through your mouth. Do this two more times. Now put the image of your inner parent outside yourself as you bring the inner child back inside your own body. Once again get a sense of what the inner child needs and wants, and what it is experiencing through you, paying particular attention to body sensations.

Allow yourself to express any feelings of disappointment in your relationships with your parents. Allow any fear, grief, or anger to emerge. Give yourself permission to express what you (as inner child) needed and wanted from your parent. Keep seeing your parent directly as you look into his or her eyes, even though it might be difficult. It is important to express aloud these unmet needs.

After you have finished dialoguing with your inner parent, take a deep breath quickly through your nose, hold it, and then let it out slowly through your mouth. Do this two more times. Put the images of your parent and child outside yourself as you continue to focus on your breathing. It is important to always be in contact with your breath.

Take a deep breath quickly through your nose, hold it, and then let it out slowly through your mouth. Repeat this two more times. As you continue to focus on your breathing permit yourself to reverse the images in your mind, so that you have externalized the child part of you and have allowed yourself to get into your parent's shoes. Take a deep breath quickly through your nose, hold it, then let it out slowly through your mouth. Allow yourself to do this two more times.

Experience the feeling(s) of your parent(s) at this moment as he/she hears what you just said. Allow your inner mother/father to talk to your child part. Let him/her talk openly from his/her own heart, describing how he/she received what you said. Allow your own parent image to fully experience his/her pain and experience that in your own body. Register the place in your body where you experience your parent's pain. Each of us carries the pain of our parents inside our bodies, just as we carry our own pain. Allow your parent to fully express to you how he/she received your message and what he/she is experiencing. Perhaps your inner parent wants to say something to you for the first time. Allow your inner child to be open and listen to your inner parent's feelings.

When your parent has fully been able to express himself/herself, continue to focus on your breathing even while you experience the parent inside you. Take a deep breath quickly through your nose, hold it, then let it out slowly through your mouth. Continue to the next part of the exercise.

Accessing the Inner Parent's Inner Child

Once again take a deep breath quickly through your nose, hold it, and then let it out slowly through your mouth. Do this two more times. Allow an image to emerge of your inner parent's inner child. What does your inner parent's inner child look like? What is he/she wearing? What kind of mood is he/she in? Allow yourself to experience your inner parent's inner child in your own body. Experience any pain that is emerging from deep inside you. Begin to allow yourself to talk from the pain of your inner parent's inner child about what his/her unmet needs are from his/her childhood.

When your inner parent's inner child has fully expressed himself/herself take a deep breath quickly through your nose, hold it, then let it out slowly through your mouth. Do this two more times as you continue the next part of the exercise.

Accessing the Inner Grandparent

Continue to focus on the sensations of your nostrils as you inhale and exhale through your nose. Once again take a deep breath quickly through your nose, hold it, then let it out slowly through your mouth. Hold the image of your inner parent's inner child deep inside your own body then continue to focus on your breathing. At the same time, allow an image of your inner grandparent outside of yourself to emerge. If you did not know your grandparent, still allow an image to emerge of what you think the grandparent might have looked like. What does your parent's parent (grandparent) look like? What is he/she wearing? What kind of expression is on his/her face? As you attach yourself to the external image of your inner grandparent, once again take a deep breath quickly through your nose, hold it, then let it out slowly through your mouth. Do this two more times.

Begin to allow your inner parent's inner child to talk from his/her heart directly to his/her parent. Perhaps you can allow your inner parent's inner child to express for the first time what he/she needed to say to his/her own parent. Let it come from the deepest place in his/her own heart. Allow yourself to do the work of your inner parent; perhaps you can help finish what your parent never finished for himself/herself. Do it for your parent's soul. Do it for your soul. Do it for all of the ancestors who perhaps are suffering in this lineage of pain.

As you allow your inner parent's inner child to focus expressing himself/herself to your inner grandparent, take a deep breath quickly through your nose and hold it, then let it out slowly through your mouth. Do this two more times as you continue this exercise. Switch images and now let your inner grandparent talk to your inner parent's inner child about his/her pain and its effect on you.

As you take a deep breath quickly through your nose, hold it, then slowly let it out through your mouth, begin to externalize the images of both your inner parent's inner child and his/her parent. See them as images outside yourself. Continue to focus on your breathing. Make sure you continue to focus on the inhale and exhale of your breathing; at the same time, let your inner parent's inner child and parent be outside yourself, then continue the exercise.

Return to the Inner Child and the Inner Parent

Continue to focus on your breath as you inhale and exhale through your nose. Take a deep breath quickly through your nose and hold it. Then let it out slowly through your mouth. Do this two more times. Allow yourself to once again see your own inner child. Take a deep breath quickly through your nose, and hold it. Then let it out slowly through your mouth. Take the image of your own inner child and continue to focus on your breathing. Once again, also allow yourself to get an image of your inner parent (mother/father). Bring this image outside yourself, as if you were standing back looking at your inner child. Continue to focus on your breathing. Now, having experienced the three generations, let your inner child talk to your inner parent.

Now let your inner child express to your parent what you are experiencing toward him/her. Express fully from your heart what it is that you are experiencing. Experience your body and what is emerging in your body. Put your hand on the area of your body where you feel yourself opening. Breathe in and out of that place. It is important to talk fully from your heart to your parent at this time. Experience what it is like to be with your parent at this time. Experience what it is like to be with your parent now, having listened to the dialogues of these exercises. See what your parent looks like as you begin to talk with him/her.

When you have finished fully expressing what you needed to say to your parent in light of these other conversations, take another deep breath quickly through your nose and hold it. Let it out slowly through your mouth. Do this two more times and go to the final exercise.

Transforming the Family Images

Close your eyes, focus your attention on your breathing as you move air in and out of your nostrils. If your attention wanders, blow a little harder through your nose and bring your concentration back to the point beneath your nose where you sense the air gently moving in and out. Take a deep breath through your nose quickly, hold it, and let it out slowly through your mouth. (Repeat three times.) Resume breathing in and out of your nostrils.

Allow an image of all of your family members to come to you, including yourself, siblings, parents, and grandparents. You may wish to include others, e.g., great-grandparents, if it seems appropriate. Put the image of everyone inside the middle of your chest (heart) and breathe in and out from that point. Hold your family in your heart.

Imagine a white, shining, glowing light above your head. Bring the light down through the top of your head, through your forehead, face, and neck. Let it fill up the center of your heart. Hold the light and your family in your heart as you breathe in and out. See what happens to the inner images. If they need to talk to one another or otherwise interact with each other, allow this to happen.

Now take a very deep breath quickly through your nose, hold it, and let it out slowly through your mouth. Do this two more times. Continue to hold your inner family in your heart. See if there is anything you now, as an adult, want to say to your inner family. Express this out loud. Express what you want to say to them as you continue to hold them in your heart. If there are any feelings that emerge, experience them as gifts and express them fully and openly.

Take a few minutes to simply relax with these images and feelings. Allow the light to move up and out and blend into the atmosphere. Let the inner family image go, knowing that you can return to this image at any time. Come back to your breathing gently through your nose. When you are ready, open your eyes.

Step 5: Evoking Compassion

As the partner doing the inner work finishes up the process of transforming his/her inner family and healing, the other partner has maintained an open caring presence. Now, having finished one or more of the previous exercises, the partners are ready to receive each other fully. The following meditation is designed to help with this process after one of them has been doing deep inner work.

Begin by making contact while continuing to remain seated in front of one another. As the person who has been doing the inner work begins to finish the process, he/she opens his/her eyes and slowly begins to receive his/her partner.

Exercise:
Both of you continue to focus on the in-breath and out-breath through your nostrils. Look deeply into each other's eyes as you have both just witnessed a very deep inner process. Look

at your partner's eyes as you continue to focus on your breathing. Each of you take a deep breath quickly through your nose, hold it, and let it out slowly through your mouth. Allow yourself to do this a few more times as you continue to look deeply into one another's eyes. Experience what is going on inside your bodies at this time. Perhaps you feel a profound opening in some area of your body, perhaps in your chest. Be open to whatever you are experiencing or to whatever is emerging. Breathe deeply through the part of your body that is beginning to open up. Perhaps you can put your hand on that area as you continue to breathe and look at your partner. Continue to be silent during this exercise. Allow whatever feelings are emerging to be there and see them as gifts.

As you continue to look into each other's eyes, the partner who has been a steady presence with openness and caring now begins to share what he or she was experiencing during this session of inner work. If you are that person, give yourself time to express all that you want to express, especially as it is coming from within your body. Share the deepest parts of your soul with your partner. The person who has just gone through the work should be in a totally receptive mode to listen to his/her partner.

As the partner who has been a steady presence with openness and caring finishes, both partners continue to focus on their breathing, inhaling and exhaling through their nostrils. Once again, take a deep breath quickly through your nose, hold it, then let it out slowly through your mouth. After a few moments, the partner who has done the inner work will have a chance to express what is happening inside of him/her as the other partner stays in a receptive mode by continuing to focus on his/her own breathing.

After you have both expressed what you needed to communicate, focus on your breathing and continue to eye-gaze. Perhaps you want to express something physically, such as hugging, holding hands, etc. Allow yourself to be able to do this while you maintain eye contact. Stay in silence for awhile.

Step 6: Grounding

The following exercise helps both partners come back to their real everyday relationship. The purpose of this last step is to share with one another more deeply what they both have learned from this experience and how they can more consciously work on their everyday relationship. The following is an exercise to finish the six steps.

> As you now have made more connection with one another, see if there is anything either of you would like to share about this experience and how it might affect your everyday relationship. Begin to share with each other how you can interact differently to embrace what has occurred during this time. For example, maybe you have a new understanding of your partner's need for assurance that you love him/her, or perhaps you now have a better understanding of why you get so upset about a particular habit of your partner's. By discussing these revelations openly, it is often possible to see new, more effective ways of interacting.

SIX BEGINNING STEPS FOR TRANSFORMING FAMILY OF ORIGIN RELATIONSHIPS

After both partners have done considerable inner and outer work, utilizing the conceptual information in this volume and the practical exercises in this section of the book, it is often useful for each partner to support the other in transforming their relationships with their own family of origin. When it is possible to do so, dialogues with one's family of origin, including parents and siblings, can help to ground the inner work with the outer realities of daily life.

Some of us have had family members die, so the following guide would be impossible to carry out. However, there are ways to achieve similar healing, which will be described later. In addition, there are cases where any efforts to carry out this further healing would be inappropriate or even dangerous. However, even though there might be tremendous resistance to doing this kind of work, it can be valuable with a family consultant trained in this type of therapy.

The following are six steps you can take to begin the process of outer family of origin transformation.

1. Compose an agenda with each family member, describing any unfinished business you have with him/her, relating to either the near or distant past. Put down unmet needs that you perceive in the past or the present. Include areas of inquiry about your early family experiences that you find confusing. It is especially important to list deep-seated pain that has not yet healed.

2. Call a family meeting. Even if your family members live very far away from one another, it is possible to arrange a weekend family meeting at a mutually agreed upon location. Just going through the process of organizing the family for such a meeting is a step toward healing the outer family relationships. It should be noted that it is much better to do this kind of process with all members of the family of origin present. Sometimes there is resistance from one or more family members. You should ask each family member to help you out by participating in this family meeting.

3. Once you have set up this family meeting, it is important to talk openly and honestly, taking responsibility for your own perceptions. It is especially important not to blame any family members for grievances you might feel. Do your best to create an atmosphere of safety, where everyone can talk openly about the history of the family as well as current interactions.

    It is important to be able to gently ask your parents more details about how they grew up including their relationship with each of their parents, siblings, and other extended family members. It is also useful to ask about your grandparents' relationship to their parents. In this way you will get a multi-dimensional picture of the ancestral patterns that have occurred through time.

    It is best to do this kind of procedure over a four-hour time period, with an hour or more break in between, on two separate days.

    Give space for others to talk when you are together. Work a great deal with your own breathing so you do not allow yourself to be overly reactive. It is important to allow family members to have enough time to be able to express themselves in a nondefensive way.

4. As you move through the process described above, see if your agenda has been covered. Remember this is a very sacred meeting and it is important to make sure that you have dealt with all the things that have been important to you during your own reflections prior to the meeting.

5. As you finish up this family meeting, make sure you express your appreciation to every one for coming and being open to this kind of dialogue.

6. Decide upon another time to be with your family and have another meeting like this. Also talk about continuing to keep the lines of communication open by telephone or through writing letters, exchanging photographs, or sharing new information or thoughts that might surface.

What do you do if your parents/siblings are dead?

1. Go to the cemetery with the agenda and speak from your heart to the grave. Express your full emotions as if the person's spirit could hear you.

2. If one or both parents have died, go to their closest friends that they knew for the longest time and talk with them openly about your parents' early life. Get to know who they were when they were younger and growing up, in their young adult years, etc. Find out what these friends really thought about them.

This particular procedure is very useful for letting go of grudges and hostility, and exonerating the parents once you achieve an emotional understanding of what has occurred in their lives.

3. It is important to complete this process with your family of origin without your partner. However, when you return, it is important to share the experience with your spouse and older children–including teenagers and young adults. This can also help in your immediate family bonding!

I hope that the introductory exercises and information in this self-help guide are useful to you. I am now in the process of writing a guidebook describing more in-depth processes for transforming the inner and outer family and thus achieving sacred connectedness.

For more information about workshops, books, and tapes about the relationship processes described here, or to find counselors who can help you continue this work in your area, contact:

Dr. Sheldon Z. Kramer
c/o the Institute for Transformations
2615 Camino Del Rio South, Suite 300
San Diego, California 92108
Tel/Fax 691-291-4465

References

Ahsen, A. (1972). *Eidetic Parents Test and Analysis.* New York: Brandon House, Inc.

Assagioli, R. (1973). *The Act of Will.* Baltimore, MD: Penguin Books, Inc.

Assagioli, R. *Psychosynthesis of the Couple.* (Unpublished transcript of talk given in Italy, August 18, 1972).

Assagioli, R. (1965a). *Psychosynthesis: A Manual of Principles and Techniques.* New York: Viking Press.

Assagioli, R. (1965b). *Psychosynthesis: Individual and Social (Some Suggested Lines of Research).* Monogram. New York: Monograph, Psychosynthesis Research Foundation.

Assagioli, R. (1933). *Dynamic Psychology and Psychosynthesis.* New York: Monograph, Psychosynthesis Research Foundation.

Baldwin, M. and Satir, V. (1987). *The Use of Self in Therapy.* Binghamton, NY: The Haworth Press.

Boszormenyi-Nagy, I. (1987). *Foundations of Contextual Therapy.* New York: Brunner Mazel.

Boszormenyi-Nagy, I. and Krasner, B. B. (1986). *Between Give and Take: A Clinical Guide to Contextual Therapy.* New York: Brunner Mazel.

Buber, M. (1970). *I and Thou.* New York: Charles Scribner's Sons.

Caveney, T. (1988). *Healing the Wounds of Adults Abused as Children: A Transpersonal Approach in Readings and Practice of Psychosynthesis.* Department of Applied Psychology, Ontario Institute for Studies in Education. Toronto, Ontario.

Charny, I. (1992). *Existential/Dialectical Marital Therapy.* New York: Brunner Mazel.

Dell, P. (1982). Beyond Homeostasis: Toward a Concept of Coherance. *Family Process, 21,* pp. 21-41.

Elliot, T. S. (1943). *Four Quartets, Burnt Norton.* London: Faber & Faber. Harcourt-Brace World, New York.

Framo, J. L. (1992). *Family of Origin Therapy: An Intergenerational Approach*. New York: Brunner Mazel.

Framo, J. L. (1982). *Exploration in Marital and Family Therapy*. Selected papers of James L. Framo, PhD. New York: Springer.

Framo, J. L. (1976). *Family of Origin as a Therapeutic Resource for Adults in Marital and Family Therapy: You Can and Should Go Home Again*. Family Process 15(2), pp. 193-210.

Framo, J. L. (1970). Symptoms from a Family Transactional Viewpoint, in *Family Therapy in Transaction*. Ackerman, N. W., Lieb, J., Pearce, J. K. (Eds.) Boston: Little Brown.

Frank, L. (1957). Research for What. *Journal of Social Issues*, Supplemental Series, No. 10.

Fuller, R. B. (1969). *Utopia or Oblivion*. New York: Bantam Books.

Heider, J. (1985). *The Tao of Leadership*. Atlanta, GA: Humanistic Limited.

Hoffman, L. (1981). *Foundations of Family Therapy*. New York: Basic Books.

Idel, M. (1991). *Kabbalah: New Perspectives*. New Haven, CT: Yale University.

James, W. (1961). *The Variety of Religious Experiences*. New York: Collier.

Johari, H. (1987). *Chakras*. Rochester, VT: Destiny Books.

Kaplan, A. (1981). *The Living Torah*. New York: Maznaim Publishing Corp.

Kramer, S. Z. (1988). *Psychosynthesis and Integrative Marital and Family Therapy*. Weiser, J., Yeomans, T. (Eds.) The Department of Applied Psychology, Ontario Institute for Studies in Education. Toronto, Ontario.

Leadbeater, C. W. (1927). *The Chakras*. Wheaton, IL: Theosophical Publishing House.

Levant, R. (1984). *Family Therapy: A Comprehensive Overview*. Englewood Cliffs, NJ: Prentice-Hall.

Levine, S. (1987). *Healing into Life and Death*. New York: Doubleday, Anchor Press.

Neil, J. R. and Kniskern, D. P. (1982). *From Psyche to System: The Evolving Therapy of Carl Whitaker*. New York: Guilford Press.

Ouspensky, P. D. (1950). *The Psychology of Man's Possible Evolution*. New York: Vintage Books.

Ouspensky, P. D. (1949). *In Search of the Miraculous: Fragments of an Unknown Teaching.* New York: Harcourt, Brace, and World, Inc.

Paul, N. L. (1966). *The Role of Mourning and Empathy in Conjoint Marital Therapy.* Palo Alto, CA: Science and Behavior Books, Inc.

Satir, V. (1988). *The New Peoplemaking.* Palo Alto, CA: Science and Behavior Books, Inc.

Satir, V. (1988). Personal communication. San Diego, CA.

Satir, V. (1978). *Your Many Faces.* Celestial Arts: Berkeley, CA.

Satir, V. (1967). *Conjoint Family Therapy: A Guide to Theory and Technique.* Palo Alto, CA: Science and Behavior Books.

Schwartz, R. (1988). *Know Thyselves.* Washington, DC: Family Therapy Networker.

Szent-Gyoergyi, A. (1974). Drive and Living Matter to Perfect Itself. *Synthesis: The Realization of the Self,* Vol. 1. Redwood City, CA: The Synthesis Press.

Trungpa, C. (1973). *Cutting Through Spiritual Materialism.* Berkeley, CA: Shambala Publications.

Tyson, R. L. and Tyson, P. (1982). A Case of PseudoNarcissistic Psychopathology: A Re-Examination of the Developmental Role of the Superego. *International Journal of Psychoanalysis, 63.*

Vargiu, J. (Ed.) (1974). Sub-Personalities. *Synthesis: The Realization of the Self.* Vol. 1. No. 1. Redwood City, CA: The Synthesis Press.

Wamboldt, F., Gurman, A., and Wamboldt, M. (1985). *Marital and Family Therapy Research: The Meaning for the Clinician.* Chapter on integrating research and clinical practice, The Family Therapy Collections. Rockville, MD: Aspen Publications.

Bibliography

(The following references were also utilized to help prepare this book).

Brown, M. Y. (1983). *The Unfolding Self.* Los Angeles, CA: Psychosynthesis Press.

Banman, J., Gerber, J., Gomori, M., and Satir, V. (1991). *The Satir Model: Family Therapy and Beyond.* Palo Alto, CA: Science and Behavior Books, Inc.

Bugental, J. (1967). *Challenges of Humanistic Psychology.* New York: McGraw-Hill.

Buhler, C. and Allen, M. (1972). *Introduction to Humanistic Psychology.* Belmont, CA: Brooks/Cole/Wadsworth Publishing.

Corey, G. (1972). *Theory and Practice of Counseling and Psychotherapy.* Monterey, CA: Brooks/Cole.

Corlis, R. B. and Rabe, P. (1969). *Psychotherapy from the Center: A Humanistic View of Change and of Growth.* Scranton, PA: International Textbook Co.

Dicks, H. (1967). *Marital Tensions.* New York: Basic Books.

Hardy, J. (1982). *A Psychology with a Soul.* New York: Routledge and Kegan Paul, Ltd.

Hart, W. (1987). *Vipassana Meditation as Taught by S. N. Goenka.* San Francisco, CA: Harper and Row.

Keeney, B. P. (1982). What is an Epistemology of Family Therapy? *Family Process,* 21:153-168.

Keeney, B. P. and Sprenkle, D. H. (1982). Ecosystemic Epistemology: Critical Implications for the Aesthetics and Pragmatics of Family Therapy. *Family Process,* 21: 1-20.

Mahrer, A. (1978). *Experiencing: A Humanistic Theory of Psychology and Psychiatry.* New York: Brunner/Mazel.

Minuchin, S. (1974). *Families and Family Therapy.* Cambridge, MA: Harvard University Press.

Minuchin, S. and Fishman, C. (1981). *Family Therapy Techniques.* Cambridge, MA: Harvard University Press.

Minuchin, S., Rosman, B. L., and Baker, L. (1978). *Psychosomatic Families: Anorexia Nervosa in Context.* Cambridge, MA: Harvard University Press.

Paul, N. and Paul, B. (1986). *A Marital Puzzle: Transgenerational Analysis in Marriage Counseling.* Revised Edition. New York: Gardner Press.

Index